Praise for
Tolstoy and the Purple Chair

"The beauty of her project lies in seeing how books intertwine with daily life, how very much they affect our moods and interactions, and, especially important for Sankovitch, how we recover and process our memories. . . . She makes reading seem accessible, relaxing, inspiring, fun."
—*Los Angeles Times*

"This graceful memoir describes a true love affair with books."
—*Boston Globe*

"Sankovitch's memoir stands as a tribute to the power of books to enrich our daily lives."
—*Christian Science Monitor*

"Nina Sankovitch has crafted a dazzling memoir that reminds us of the most primal function of literature—to heal, to nurture, and to connect us to our truest selves."
—Thrity Umrigar, author of *The Space Between Us*

"A beautifully fluid, reflective, and astute memoir that gracefully combines affecting family history with expert testimony about how books open our minds to 'the complexity and entirety of the human experience.' Sankovitch's reading list in all its dazzling variety is top-notch."
—*Booklist*

"[*Tolstoy and the Purple Chair*] digs deep into that near-mystical connection between a reader and an author—that startling feeling that you are channeling someone you have never met. . . . A gripping and inspiring book."
—*Connecticut Post*

"[Sankovitch's] deeply moving memoir artfully intertwines her immigrant family's history with the universal themes of hope, resilience, and memory. *Tolstoy and the Purple Chair* celebrates not only the healing power of literature but its ability to connect us to the best of ourselves—and each other."
—*American Way* magazine

TOLSTOY

AND

THE

PURPLE

CHAIR

TOLSTOY

AND

THE

PURPLE

CHAIR

My Year of Magical Reading

NINA

SANKOVITCH

HARPER PERENNIAL

NEW YORK • LONDON • TORONTO • SYDNEY • NEW DELHI • AUCKLAND

HARPER ● PERENNIAL

A hardcover edition of this book was published in 2011 by HarperCollins Publishers.

HarperCollins books may be purchased for educational, business, or sales promotional use. For information please write: Special Markets Department, HarperCollins Publishers, 10 East 53rd Street, New York, NY 10022.

Photograph on page v courtesy of the author

FIRST HARPER PERENNIAL EDITION PUBLISHED 2012.

Designed by Fritz Metsch

The Library of Congress has cataloged the hardcover edition as follows:
Sankovitch, Nina.
Tolstoy and the purple chair : my year of magical reading / by Nina Sankovitch.
p.cm.
ISBN 978-0-06-199984-0 (hardback)
1. Sankovitch, Nina—
Books and reading. 2. Books and reading—United States. I. Title.
Z1003.2.S26 2011
028'.8—dc22   2010052855

ISBN 978-0-06-199985-7 (pbk.)

12 13 14 15 16 OV/RRD 10 9 8 7 6 5 4 3 2 1

In Memory of Anne-Marie Sankovitch
and for Our Family

We need the books that affect us like a disaster,
that grieve us deeply, like the death of someone
we loved more than ourselves, like being banished
into forests far from everyone, like a suicide.
A book must be the ax for the frozen sea inside us.
——FRANZ KAFKA,
letter to Oskar Pollak, January 27, 1904

A book is a garden, an orchard, a storehouse, a
party, a company by the way, a counselor,
a multitude of counselors.
——HENRY WARD BEECHER,
Proverbs from Plymouth Pulpit

CONTENTS

CONTENTS

TOLSTOY

AND

THE

PURPLE

CHAIR

Everywhere I have sought rest and not found it,
except sitting in a corner by myself with a little
book.

THOMAS À KEMPIS

IN SEPTEMBER 2008 MY HUSBAND, JACK, AND I WENT AWAY
for a weekend, leaving our four kids in the care of my parents.
We went by car from suburban Connecticut out to the Atlantic beaches of Long Island. We had a Windsurfer lashed to our
roof and a bike shoved in the back on top of our few bags filled
with clothes and books, enough for three days away. Our vacation weekend was my present to Jack in honor of his fifti-
eth birthday. I had signed him up for an advanced windsurfing
workshop, booked us into a hotel off Montauk Highway, and
finagled a dinner reservation at a local hot spot that was notori-
ously difficult to get into.

On our first day there, while Jack was out riding the wind,
I took off on my bicycle. I headed east to Montauk, carrying a
book in my bike basket, *Dracula* by Bram Stoker, along with a
water bottle and a packet of chocolate. I rode the winding hills
of old Montauk Highway, a road that stays close to the ocean
shoreline, buffered only by scrubland, fir trees, and cliffs. After a
half hour or so, I stopped my bike by an opening cutting through
the brush. There, down a little path, I found a perfect spot. A

wooden bench stood rooted to the edge of the cliff, faded to a light and shiny gray by sand, wind, and rain, as if buffed and polished. Sheltered from the sun by an overhanging scrub tree and facing out over the Atlantic Ocean, the bench was both solitary and encompassing. I could sit there and be alone, and then look up and see the world unfolding before me in a cascade of blue-and-white waves and glittering sunlight over water. I leaned my bike against a rock, took the book, chocolate, and water out of the basket, and sat down on the bench to read.

I spent my day on that bench, getting up occasionally to stretch and at one point, riding off in search of a bathroom and lunch. But I returned to read again, caught up in the gothic journey of Dracula from Transylvania to England, and back again to Transylvania. I traveled over mountains and past crazed villagers, dodging vampires and accompanied by the good guys, Jonathan Harker, Van Helsing, and Mina. We were fighting to save the world from vampire takeover.

The suddenly shifting cold breezes of early evening brought me back to where I was, sitting on a bench on a Montauk cliff. I had to return to the hotel and get ready for our dinner out. On the bike ride home I stopped at a farmer's market and picked up some apples, a chunk of blue cheese, and a loaf of bread. I stopped at a liquor store for red wine and then swerved my way to the hotel, my bike basket overflowing.

Jack wasn't back yet. Great, I thought to myself. I won't get ready for dinner; I'll just keep reading. To stave off hunger, I cut some cheese for myself, loaded it onto a crust of the bread, and poured out a generous slug of wine. With my hand curled around the glass, I continued to read. Van Helsing was hot on the trail of Count Dracula, closing in on the bloodsucking aristocrat.

I was asleep on my book, drained wineglass on the floor and half the entire blue cheese consumed, when Jack got back from his windsurfing. I didn't even feel him as he slipped in on the couch beside me. When I woke up at ten thirty, he was there behind me, snoring away, smelling salty and sweaty. Our dinner reservation was long past. I wriggled into an upright position, poured myself another glass of wine, and finished off *Dracula*.

The next day I realized I had done it. I had read a book in one day. And a very hefty book at that, more than four hundred pages in all. Of course there had been other days in my life when I'd devoured a book in one sitting or in paced feastings over the course of one day. But this book on this day had been a test for me. And I knew now that I was ready. I was ready to read a book a day for one year.

When Jack took off after breakfast for another day of windsurfing, I rode my bike over to the restaurant we'd skipped out on the night before. I arrived sweaty and dusty, eager to explain to the maître d' how, last night, we had just slept through our reservation. She was a tall, statuesque beauty, and she laughed as I told her my story.

"I've never heard that one before," she said as she penciled us in with a star for eight o'clock.

At dinner that night, I raised my glass of Italian white, just poured out by our efficient waiter, and looked Jack in the eye. I had his attention.

"To my year of reading," I announced.

"You're really going to do it?" he asked.

I nodded.

"A book a day? How about a book a week?" he asked.

No, I needed to read a book a day. I needed to sit down and sit still and read. I had spent the last three years running and racing, filling my life and the lives of everyone in my family with activity and plans and movement, constant movement.

But no matter how much I crammed into living, and no matter how fast I ran, I couldn't get away from the grief and the pain.

It was time to stop running. It was time to stop doing anything and everything. It was time to start reading.

"To your year of reading, then," Jack seconded, and clinked his glass with mine. "May it be everything you want it to be, and more."

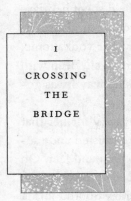

I

———

CROSSING
THE
BRIDGE

*It is from knowing that he is dead that he wants
to protect his son. As long as I live, he thinks, let
me be the one who knows! By whatever act of will
it takes, let me be the thinking animal plunging
through the air.*

J. M. COETZEE,
The Master of Petersburg

MY SISTER WAS FORTY-SIX YEARS OLD WHEN SHE DIED. During the few months between her diagnosis and her death, I traveled back and forth from home in Connecticut to New York City to see her. I usually came in by train. On the train I could read. I read for the same reasons I've always done it, for pleasure and escape. But now I was also reading to forget—for just a half hour or so—the reality of what my sister was going through. She had been diagnosed with bile duct cancer. The cancer advanced relentlessly and quickly. It left pain, helplessness, and fear in its wake.

I always carried with me on the train a book or two for Anne-Marie. After finding out about her cancer, I'd done a furious Internet search—everyone hit by the diagnosis does it—and I'd read that reading funny books can help fight the illness. Escapist books would also help with fighting off the evil cells, but the articles advised me to lay off any heavy reading material. So I brought in Woody Allen and Steve Martin for Anne-Marie, and I also brought in lots of murder mysteries. Murder mysteries involve death, and none of us wanted to think about death, but Anne-Marie had always used mysteries to unwind and relax. As an art historian, she'd spent her days poring over dense texts and examining architectural details, plans, and photos. Mysteries were her candy, her vodka tonic, her bubble bath. She loved mysteries rich in detail, deep with atmosphere, and dark in motive. There was no way I was going to deny her now.

One day in mid-April I brought in a mystery for her that I had not yet read. Carl Hiaasen's books are twisted and raucous. I was sure he'd be a good antidote to pain and fear. On the train I laid aside my own book and opened up *Basket Case*. It was very funny and full of atmosphere, crazy South Florida atmosphere. But I quickly realized that the book hit too close to home. The main character, Jack Tagger, is certain he will die in his forty-sixth year. My sister had to make it to forty-seven—she had to—and I could not let any doubt creep in. I read the book furtively and quickly and never gave it to Anne-Marie to read.

If I had known for certain that my sister would not make it to forty-seven, would I have moved to New York City to be closer to her, leaving my husband and four boys in Connecticut to fend for themselves? No, I doubt it. Anne-Marie wanted to see me in doses. I was the youngest of three sisters, and Anne-Marie was the oldest, with Natasha in between. All our lives, Anne-Marie told us when she wanted us around and when she wanted us gone, and we listened.

We were raised in Evanston, Illinois, by immigrant parents. They had come to the United States for new opportunities, leaving all family and support behind. We made our own tight-knit unit of five. We had plenty of friends, but my sisters and I felt like aliens most of the time. Our family was different from other families. Our house had more books, more art, and more dust than anyone else's. We had no relatives living close by, no grandparents for the holidays, no aunts for baby-sitting, no cousins to play with. Our parents had strong—and in the case of my father, scary—foreign accents. Our mother worked, first as a grad student and then as a full-time professor, from the time I entered kindergarten. My sisters and I were the only kids from our neighborhood who ate lunch in school, and we were the only kids in the whole entire Midwest who had sliced green peppers and hard red pears packed alongside the more ordinary white-bread sandwiches and Twinkies.

Books were a part of my family's life, present in every room and read every night by both parents, to themselves and to us. My mother read to us girls in the living room. I loved lying back on the rug and looking up at the cracked ceiling, listening to the stories of King Arthur and the Round Table. Sir Gawain was my favorite, although he definitely caused my hang-ups over boys later; they were much too easily seduced compared to Gawain. The beautiful Lady Bertilak approaches Gawain day after day, but he never gives in to her kisses. The boys I would grow up to kiss gave in without any effort at all, and yet it was my reputation on the line, not theirs. After King Arthur came the animals of *The Wind in the Willows*. Life in the English countryside post-Camelot seemed so dull. The so-called grand adventure of Mole and Rat was really just a series of mishaps, and the final battle made me yawn. I could not get excited about invading weasels and a slimy toad.

Sunday afternoons were also spent reading, indoors in the winter months, and outside in our small backyard in the summer. It was not until I was in high school and had an American boyfriend that we spent a Sunday afternoon watching a football game. It was the Super Bowl. A surprisingly chivalrous-for-the-day Dan Cromer explained the whole game to my parents and me. But that was the last time he spoke to me, later ignoring me in the hallways at school and never calling back when I left messages at his home. If I didn't understand football, what good could I be?

The first book I can remember claiming as my own was one I stole from the Lincolnwood Elementary School library. It was *My Mother Is the Most Beautiful Woman in the World* by Becky Reyher. I still have that book today. It's on a bookshelf in my bedroom, alongside other favorites from childhood, and it still has its library due-date card: December 6, 1971. I loved that book and just could not return it when the date came. I don't remember if I paid the lost fee.

In the book, Varya, a young Ukrainian girl, becomes separated from her mother while they're working in the fields. People from a neighboring village who are out harvesting wheat try to help Varya find her mother, but the only description the child can give is that her mother "is the most beautiful woman in the world." The villagers send messengers to all the local farms, asking them to send the most beautiful women back to the clearing where Varya waits, sobbing. One by one, beautiful women are paraded before the little girl, but she shakes her head at each one, sobbing harder and harder. And then a woman comes running up: "Her face was big and broad, and her body even larger. Her eyes were little pale slits between a great lump of a nose. The mouth was almost toothless." She is Varya's mother, and the mother and child are reunited: "The smile Varya had longed for was once again shining upon her." That story still brings me to tears. It conveyed to me as a nine-year-old, as it does today, the innocent and resplendent love between parent and child.

My mother really was and still is the most beautiful woman in the world, and Anne-Marie was too: the two most beautiful women in the world, in one family. On the day my sister died, she had been feeling well enough to sit up in bed and put on eyeliner, mascara, and lipstick. She never needed that stuff to look good, but it added glamour, even when she was so ill. She let me brush her hair that day, lovely dark blond hair. She had been worried it would fall out in treatment, but we never got that far. We would have traded a lifetime of hair from all of our heads just to have the chance to fight her illness. But the bile duct cancer moved too fast. Treatment turned out to be only a torture, and never a cure.

I wasn't planning on going in to see Anne-Marie the day she died. I'd been to visit her every day since she'd been readmitted to the hospital in early May. On a beautiful spring morning she'd woken to a belly swollen up to horrific proportions. Her system was shutting down, and bile and liquid were backing up. She hung on at home, hoping her insides would start working again, but by evening she knew she had to go back to the hospital. I was out with Jack, celebrating our thirteenth wedding anniversary, when I got the call. We were walking by the river that winds along behind the main street of our town. I closed my phone and walked away from Jack, going out on the pier that juts into the marshes at the river's edge. It was low tide, and the smell of salt and muck and decay mixed with the soft, warm spring breeze. I closed my eyes and cried.

The next day I took the train into the city, then walked the thirty blocks up to New York–Presbyterian. And the next day I took the train again, and the next day again.

On the day my father turned eighty years old, Anne-Marie was feeling up to a chocolate truffle and a sip of champagne. I continued to go in every day, and Anne-Marie continued to get better, in increments and with some backtracking. In the last few days she had been eating more, and talking and laughing easily. She had taken to wearing two pairs of reading glasses, one propped on top of the other on her head, just in case. She seemed ready for anything.

I considered taking a day at home to catch up on loads of unwashed laundry and unpaid bills, but Jack urged me to go in and see her.

"Just drive in with me for the morning. You'll be back in time for the boys." The boys were my older children, Peter, Michael, and George. The youngest of my four, Martin, was still in pre-K and with me for the day. It would cheer my mother up to see him. She could take him to the playground by the hospital, and I could go in for a quick visit with Anne-Marie.

The pants I wore into the city that day were loose on me. In the past month, I'd stopped eating meals regularly and had put an end to wine at night. Just one glass led to crying. Even if the kids were in bed, I didn't want them to wake up and hear me sobbing. The kindness and patience they'd shown me had already exceeded what any kid should have had to muster. Peter had gone in with me one Sunday to see Anne-Marie. When we left her hospital room, he put his arm around me and said, "I love you, Mom." Eleven years old, and he was comforting me.

Just a few days ago, I'd cried to Michael that Martin was lucky because he was too young to understand that Anne-Marie was dying. Michael answered, "No, Mommy, he's not lucky. He's not lucky at all because he's never going to know Anne-Marie like we do." Michael remembered his own sleepovers, Scrabble games, and hours of Lego with her. Anne-Marie was always the bad Lego guy, out to ruin the world created by the good Lego guys. Bad Lego guy was always defeated in the end.

I stopped in a store to buy a belt for my falling pants. I wanted something really attention getting. That was my job with Anne-Marie when she was in the hospital: to get her attention, to get her to laugh or to whip out a sharp, smart comment.

Proof that she was still with us. I told her funny and startling stories about my kids. I wore new and strange combinations of clothes, each day crazier than the day before. Anne-Marie smiled and laughed when she saw me. She forgot for a minute that she was dying. I would do anything to give her that minute.

So I picked out a shockingly ugly pink-and-white-and-Day-Glo-orange-striped belt, cinched up my old jeans, and went to do the exchange with my mother. She'd take Martin, and I'd take the elevator to the eighth floor.

We had a great visit. Anne-Marie was animated and involved as soon as I came in the room. She gave my belt a well-deserved insult. Leaning over, she took the book I'd brought in for her, *Runaway*, a collection of short stories by Alice Munro. She pulled down a pair of glasses from atop her head to read from a story she'd opened to. Later I read the stories and fixated on the line, "She hopes as people who know better hope for undeserved blessings, spontaneous remissions, things of that sort." We all hoped that way. Anne-Marie never had the time to read all the books I'd brought her. She read just one page of the Munro and then closed it up and added it to her pile.

I brushed back her hair from her face; she was lovely. My parents had never compared us as kids. To them we were all smart and beautiful. But we knew the truth: Anne-Marie was the beauty, Natasha was the good girl, and I was the pudgy, funny one.

Three girls, all of us different, but all of us loved books. From the time we could toddle, we toddled toward books. When I was just three years old, the three of us would walk together to the library bookmobile. It stopped at a corner just a few blocks away from our house. In *Fahrenheit 451*, Ray Bradbury describes books smelling "like nutmeg or some spice from a foreign land." For me, books do have a spicy smell, but it is a local spice, soothing and familiar. It is the smell of the bookmobile, a mixture of musty pages and warm bodies. We crowded in along the shelves, looking for what we wanted along the lower brackets; the ones above were for the grown-up books. Anchored shelves in the middle of the van were for new releases, with a slot to the side for returning due books. At home we were expected to keep track of our library books and to get them back on time. Anne-Marie and I were usually late, Natasha never.

Piles of books were stacked along the windowsill of Anne-Marie's hospital room, gifts from friends and from family. I was borrowing as many as I brought in. Anne-Marie had just introduced me to the writer Deborah Crombie and her sleuths, Duncan Kincaid and Gemma James. She reread the series while I worked my way through, virgin and loving it. I was in the middle of *All Shall Be Well*. The title held out hope, and when I had seen the book there on the hospital sill, I'd asked to borrow it. Anne-Marie had said yes, but said she wanted it back. We were all still planning for more time.

My father was there that morning, along with Marvin, Anne-Marie's husband. Marvin slept in Anne-Marie's room every night, and so he was tired every day. Sleep wasn't easy wrapped around a woman in a hospital bed who was hooked up to all kinds of bags and tubes. I sought to make him laugh, and my father too. It was important that I play the fool and jester. When we laughed, we forgot that we were in a room with a woman who had little hope left. The optimism of forgetting stayed with us, allowing us to make plans. Anne-Marie ate her Jell-O, and we all imagined that tomorrow she'd move up to something more solid. We talked about driving out to Bellport, Anne-Marie's house by the sea, as soon as she got out of the hospital. I promised to get her started on a new mystery series

I'd discovered, written by M. C. Beaton and starring the un-ambitious but ruggedly adorable Hamish Macbeth, a police-man from the Scottish Highlands. I offered to bring in a couple of titles on my next visit. Anne-Marie looked skeptical—pre-ferring London to the Scottish countryside—but I assured her that Beaton's eccentric characters more than made up for the rural atmosphere. We all laughed again.

When Anne-Marie became tired, her eyes would close half-way and her words would stop midsentence. That was my cue to leave, to let her rest with her books and the newspaper. I kissed her and told her I loved her and I'd see her tomorrow. "Tell me again about Martin's new shoes," she asked, her eyes opening wide for a minute. I told her about my three-year-old's new shoes, pink Merrells. He loved everything pink. She nodded.

"See you tomorrow," she said.

One hour later, my sister died. She handed my mother a folded-back piece of her *New York Times*, said, "Read that. It's interesting," and then attempted to rise from the bed. Blood gurgled up from her throat, and she fell back. The nurse pushed past my mother, and told her to go find Marvin, who had gone out into the hall. But it was too late. Anne-Marie was gone.

I was driving over the Henry Hudson Bridge with Martin belted into his car seat behind me when my cell phone rang. I carried it wedged between my legs so I could answer it quickly, and I did. Jack interrupted my words about what a great visit I'd had.

"Nina, you have to come back."

"Why? Why do I have to come back?" I started to feel sick to my stomach. Jack didn't answer me.

"Tell me, why do I have to come back? What's wrong?"

"Anne-Marie is dead."

I screamed. And screamed again. I pulled the car over and continued screaming, my throat raking itself bloody and sore. Martin sat speechless behind me. He must have been terrified. When I stopped screaming, I started crying. I turned the car around and drove back into New York City, back to the hospital.

Anne-Marie had been laid out in the bed with her arms crossed over her body. A cloth was wrapped around her head, holding her mouth closed. My mother stood beside her, crying quietly, holding on to the cloth that covered her body. Marvin paced the room. Jack talked with the nurse, who was urging us to move out so that the body could be taken down to the morgue. I'd left Martin in the waiting room with another nurse, drawing pictures. Natasha cried on the couch, sitting next to my father. She held his arm as tears trembled down his cheeks, shaking along with his body as he weaved back and forth. "Three in one night," he kept mumbling to himself, repeating over and over, "Three in one night."

I tried to pull my mother away from the bed. "Let's go, Mommy. That's not Anne-Marie anymore."

"Yes, she is," my mother corrected me. "Yes, this is Anne-Marie." She turned back to my sister, back to stroking her cheek, holding on to her hand above the sheet.

But that body was no longer my sister. Anne-Marie was gone. We could still have her with us in words and memories and photos. She was ours to remember and talk about and dream about. But she was gone from herself, never to know or feel or talk or dream, ever again. That was the first horror of losing Anne-Marie: she lost herself. She lost life and all its wondrous, incalculable possibilities. While the rest of us would live on, she would not. It was all over for her. Even if I thought the spirit of her person might persist in another dimension or another space—and how could I know this or deny this?—her place on earth as she felt it, tasted it, knew it, was gone. Lights-out, over, forever.

As horrible as losing her life was, there was even more horror for me in that Anne-Marie knew it was happening. I had failed to protect Anne-Marie from knowing her death was coming. All my books and foolery and stupid clothes could not stop her from knowing. She was too smart to ignore the truth that came with the doctors' visits and the test results and what she felt inside.

From the time she was a child, Anne-Marie had used intelligence and intuition to see through lies and bullshit. She quit the Brownies after two weeks because the mothers running the troop just could not explain the arts and crafts. Anne-Marie did not see the point of making lanyards, and until the mothers could justify the wrapping of plastic strings around and around, she was out of there. As an adult, she eviscerated long-held assumptions about Renaissance architecture and constructed whole new ways of looking at societal and civic impacts on church construction in the fifteenth and sixteenth centuries. She knew Jack was the man for me before I did, and she knew my kids would be beautiful before they were even born. She had the very rare ability to see and understand all sides of any situation or problem or endeavor, clearly and without prejudgment. When her doctors used clinical terms and a calm, quiet tone to discuss the usual course of bile duct cancer and the possibilities of treatment, she understood, long before any of us did, that the treatment was palliative only. She felt the cancer moving inside, strangling life out of her with every step. Death was on its way.

Only once did I see my sister break down during the three months of her illness. One Saturday in March I went in to see Anne-Marie at her apartment while Jack took the boys to the Museum of Natural History. We sat next to each other on the couch in her book-lined study. I remember how suddenly she reached over to hold on to me, to hug me close to her, pulling me up into her thick gray cardigan so that my face was buried in her hair and her face was buried in my hair. She wanted to be close, but she could not look me in the eye as she said what she knew.

"It is so unfair."

The words filtered through to me. It was unfair that she had to die. She said it only once. I understood. I held her to me, and there was nothing I could say, except over and over again that I loved her. I have that gray sweater now, and I wear it in the winter. I know how unfair life is. But while we all know life is not fair, Anne-Marie knew it more. And it horrifies me that I could not take that knowledge away from her and bear it myself, for her.

In *The Master of Petersburg*, author J. M. Coetzee imagines Dostoyevsky feeling the same horror. Dostoyevsky's son has just died in a fall. The death saddens Dostoyevsky, but what haunts him is that his son knew his own death was coming and there was nothing he could do to spare his son that knowledge: "What he cannot bear is the thought that, for the last fraction of the last instant of his fall, Pavel knew that nothing could save him, that he was dead. . . . It is from knowing that he is dead that he wants to protect his son. As long as I live, he thinks, let me be the one who knows! By whatever act of will it takes, let me be the thinking animal plunging through the air."

I was the one left knowing, but I knew too late, and my knowledge never helped my sister. What good could my knowing do me now? I had more questions every day, and no wisdom to provide the answers. What had my father meant with his repeated incantation of "three in one night"? How could I have denied my mother so soon, telling her that body was not her daughter? How could I explain death to my children without taking away their innocence? How would any of us ever be able to go back out into the world and live, smile, talk, plan ever again?

The questions formed in my mind, and no answers came. Piling up, one on top of the other, the questions came down heavier and heavier until my head ached and my back bowed from the weight. The questions dug in deep, anchoring me to the fact and to the sorrow of losing my oldest sister.

Sorrow for me became the ceaseless pain of knowing I could not protect my sister from death. All I wanted was to be the one who knew: "Let me be the one who knows!" I wanted to be the one who bore the death, and leave all the others, Anne-Marie included, free to go on.

2

RETURN TO THE BOOKMOBILE

Words are alive and literature becomes an escape,
not from, but into living.

CYRIL CONNOLLY,
The Unquiet Grave

AFTER ANNE-MARIE'S DEATH, I BECAME A WOMAN OF TWO parts. One part of me was still in her hospital room, the afternoon she died. The room with its reclined bed, easy chair, TV, and piles of books. The silver tripods holding bags of fluid, painkiller, and horrible brown liquid that drained from my sister's blocked stomach. The tray overflowing with newspapers and Jell-O packs. The balled-up socks I'd brought in that were too small to pull onto my sister's swollen and blue feet. The brush with strands of dark blond hair.

Then there was the other part of me, the part that left the hospital room at a gallop and never looked back, for fear of what I would see. I began a race the day Anne-Marie died, a race away from death, away from my father's pain and my mother's sorrow, away from loss and confusion and despair. I was scared of dying, scared of losing my own life. I was scared of what dying did to family left behind, the loneliness and the helplessness. The horrible second-guessing: Should we have tried other doctors, other treatments, other methods?

I was scared of living a life not worth the living. Why did I deserve to live when my sister had died? I was responsible now for two lives, my sister's and my own, and, damn, I'd better live well. I had to live hard and live fully. I was going to live double if my sister couldn't live at all. I was going to live double because I had to die too, one day, and I didn't want to miss anything. I set myself to a faster and faster speed. I drove myself through action and plans and trips and activities. I wanted to make my parents smile again and keep my kids from thinking about death. I wanted to love Jack and walk for miles with Natasha. I had to make up for everything that everyone around me lost when Anne-Marie died.

I began coaching Martin's soccer team, and offered to help out with Peter's Lego robotics team. I took on leadership of a PTA committee. I set myself on a fitness regime and went to see every doctor with any authority over a region of the body: ear, nose, and throat; vagina and breast; eye; knee (arthritis from an old soccer injury); and colon. Two years before Anne-Marie died, I'd quit working, and there was no way I was going back to work now. I had to be available to everyone in my family, from the youngest (Martin) to the oldest (my father). I tried to anticipate every need and offer all kinds of encouragement.

Three years at increasing speed, and then I realized I couldn't do it. I couldn't get away from the sorrow. I could not guarantee my own life span, or anyone else's. I could not make everyone around me safe and happy. My forty-sixth birthday was looming, and suddenly all I could think about was how my sister had died at forty-six. I had always heard that middle age catches a person wondering, Is this all there is? But for me it was the question posed by my sister's death three years earlier that banged harder and harder against my brain.

Why do I deserve to live?

My sister had died, and I was alive. Why was I given the life card, and what was I supposed to do with it?

I had to stop running. The answer to those questions would not be found in constant activity. I had to stand still and take time to merge my two parts back together again, the one caught in my sister's hospital room and the one stuck on a treadmill set to the highest speed. There was a link between the life I had before and the life I had now. My sister was the link. In that link I would find my answers.

I looked back to what the two of us had shared. Laughter. Words. Books.

Books. The more I thought about how to stop and get myself back together as one sane, whole person, the more I thought about books. I thought about escape. Not running to escape but reading to escape. Cyril Connolly, twentieth-century writer and critic, wrote that "words are alive and literature becomes an escape, not from, but into living." That was how I wanted to use books: as an escape back to life. I wanted to engulf myself in books and come up whole again.

I had been reading a lot in the three years since my sister died, but the books I chose were closer to torture than to comfort. The raw clarity of pain in Joan Didion's *Year of Magical Thinking*, her account of her husband's sudden death, intensified my own sorrow. Then there were the weeks I read only the ridiculous but sweet and addictive Aunt Dimity mysteries by Nancy Atherton. Aunt Dimity may be dead, but she still has the power to communicate her very wise advice to the living. How I wished—I cried!—for such communion with Anne-Marie.

I read all the Barbara Cleverly novels starring Joe Sandilands because Anne-Marie had read them all and told me they were great, and I wanted to know her again; I wanted to understand what she loved and what she found worthy of her hard-to-get respect. I reread one of her favorite books from when she was just a little kid, *Danny Dunn and the Homework Machine* by Jay Williams and Raymond Abrashkin. I had her Scholastic Book Club copy, priced at fifty cents but priceless now with "Anne-Marie Sankovitch" written in her handwriting on the inner flap. The last pages of the book had been lost over the years. I hunted down a replacement copy on the Internet so I could finish the reading of it.

I've used books my whole life for wisdom, for succor, and for escape. The summer before I entered middle school was the year I began to step away from childhood and toward who I would become as an adult. I suffered my first heartbreak, my first death up close, and my first inkling that life was just not fair. *Harriet the Spy* by Louise Fitzhugh held me together during those bewildering and scary rites of passage.

The summer began with my best friend, Carol, moving away from my neighborhood. Throughout elementary school Carol and I played together after school, almost every day. I'd first noticed Carol in kindergarten. I'd noticed her because she had a thick, soft, woolly bath mat for her napping rug while I had a rag rug, thin and flat like a pancake. Carol allowed me to place my rug near hers during naptime, and even to rest my head on a fluffy corner of her mat. We became best friends, walking to and from school together every day. Afternoons were spent playing together at her house or mine. Fifth grade was our *Gilligan's Island* year. Every day after school we would watch a *Gilligan's Island* rerun on TV and then we would play, pretending we were the ones cast away on a deserted island. I was always Ginger, and Carol was always Mary Ann, and the gist of our play was how we both loved the Professor. All our adventures on the deserted island revolved around the Professor. Because we were friends, best friends, we both got to have him in our afternoon games, using the doorjambs of rooms as stand-ins for the straight and narrow Professor. We kissed those doorjambs and laughed like hyenas. The thought that he might prefer one or the other, Ginger or Mary Ann, or might find someone else (ha—not on a deserted island), never occurred to us. We were prepubescent, innocent, and happy.

And then one day we weren't. Carol moved to a street far enough away that we could no longer just drop in on each other. Our play had to be planned and involved parents and cars and schedules. When summer vacation began, I was left in the old neighborhood with old—but not best—friends while Carol moved on to new friends. And, very quickly, she found a new best friend. Carol was no longer interested in me or the Professor.

The only way I got through the loneliness of that summer was by reading *Harriet the Spy*. Harriet became my new best friend. I could not play Gilligan's Island alone, but I could spy on my own. In fact, that was one of Harriet's rules of spying! Suddenly, being alone was not so bad. I began to carry around a notebook and scribble my thoughts down in it. I didn't do much actual spying. My sisters caught on quickly to what I was up to with my notebook, my dime-store binoculars, and the copy of *Harriet the Spy* that I always had with me. They told my mother, and she gave me a quiet lecture on respecting the privacy of our neighbors. No big deal. I was more interested in writing my own thoughts in my notebook than in spying on boring suburban neighbors. Reading and rereading *Harriet the Spy* brought me somewhere new, to a place where a girl my age lived, a girl who loved to read and scribble and eat peculiar foods just like me. Harriet took me with her to her world, a place where Ole Golly talked to us kids as if we were smart and big, telling us all about writers like Henry James and Dostoyevsky and making them sound wonderful. It was a place of solitary freedom and tomato sandwiches. When Harriet found herself in deep trouble with her friends, I didn't want her to work things out with them. I wanted her to be alone, like I was.

In mid-July of that summer my mother and I left for Belgium. My grandmother was in the final stages of cancer, and my mother was going to care for her. I was brought along because at age ten I was too young to be left unsupervised at home, and maybe because my mother had noticed my sadness over losing Carol. She wanted to keep an eye on me. My father and older sisters would join us in August, when we would head east to visit relatives in Poland. I was happy to be flying away to Belgium, unaware of just how ill my grandmother was. I sat on the plane feeling very safe, with my mother beside me, and my copy of *Harriet the Spy*, my notebook, and my stuffed Piglet—beloved Piggy—anchored in between our seats.

I remember sitting on the bed where my grandmother lay, very ill but still smiling, still eager to spoil me. "When I'm better, we'll go shopping, yes?" she asked in her lovely voice, her English accented and slightly warbling. But she didn't get better. I don't remember anyone telling me that she had died. I just remember my aunt taking me to buy clothes for the funeral, a plain blue skirt, white jersey, black shoes.

Just before the funeral I developed a brain-splitting headache, so bad that I vomited again and again. My grandfather, a doctor, gave me a sedative that made me feel better, and I went to the funeral. I sat beside my mother, waiting alone on the bench while she went up to the casket. My mother cried, the only time I saw her cry that summer, but I don't remember crying—I was half numb with the headache medication.

In the days that followed, my mother took me all over Antwerp. We walked everywhere. It was wonderful being with her, going to the zoo, down to the port by the river, and to Rubens's house, filled with his paintings. I liked the blue-and-white tiles encircling the kitchen fireplace in Rubens's house, each tile presenting a different tiny scene from life. Afternoons we would sit at a café and share sugared waffles, my mother drinking coffee while I had hot cocoa. I would scribble away in my notebook, poems and thoughts and notes about what we'd seen that day. Harriet was always with me. My mother and aunt bought me new books to read, but I always went back to favorite pages of *Harriet the Spy*, like the scene where Harriet describes how she first began to listen in on other people's conversations while drinking her egg cream at the counter of her local diner. I had no idea what an egg cream was, but I understood the fun when Harriet "would play a game and not look at the people until from listening to them she had decided what they looked like. Then she would turn around and see if she were right."

My mother was good at eavesdropping, but I was even better, picking up the English conversations going on around us in those cafés and reporting the funny stuff I heard. Then my mother and I would both turn around and peek at the overheard couples and families, and laugh behind our hands.

In August my father and sisters arrived in Belgium. We left for Poland, driving eastward across Europe to visit brothers my father hadn't seen for thirty years, since World War II. There was a dramatic change as we drove into Eastern Europe from Germany. Well cared for brick and stone buildings, clean cobblestone streets, and the sleek Autobahn gave way to a drab and gray symmetry of cement block buildings interspersed with crumbling roads and long banks of fields being worked by rusty machinery or by hand.

We stayed first with my father's oldest brother, who lived and worked on an old estate that was now a large flower nursery. Despite the shabbiness of the once-grand house, the property was impressive, with gorgeous wide rows of flowers spreading out in all directions. There was also a small vegetable garden next to the house. We ate salads of fresh tomatoes and cucumbers during long meals with everyone smiling and talking in a language that, for once, my mother didn't understand. She just nodded and smiled, and we girls followed along.

We drove on after a few days to Kraków, to visit another brother. His two-room house was jam-packed with vases, photographs, bowls, paintings, and books. Mismatched pieces of furniture pushed up against each other, fighting for space. Again there were long meals (bread and sausage) and lots of smiling and talking in a language that I didn't understand. I stuck to talking with my sisters and rereading *Harriet the Spy*. At night, my sisters and I slept in the back room of the house, sharing the larger of the two beds with our aunt. My parents slept in the other bed, a narrow twin.

My aunt was a large woman, and when she shifted on the bumpy mattress, my sisters and I tumbled and rolled. Anne-Marie reached out with her arm to hold me in the bed. I might have fallen onto the floor without her steadying hand. I clutched Anne-Marie with one hand and held tightly on to Piggy with the other. None of us girls slept much.

We left Poland, driving north into East Germany, with the idea of crossing back over into Western Europe through Berlin. But tourists were supposed to enter West Berlin from the south, avoiding East Berlin altogether. The reason for this became obvious as we drove through the streets of East Berlin. Our shiny Western car stuck out like a display of fireworks in a gloomy sky. The few people we passed on the crumbling streets stopped to stare at us. All talk in the car ceased, and we made our way silently along entire blocks of bombed-out buildings, under the dim lights of weak streetlamps. Only Checkpoint Charlie, the crossing point to West Berlin, was lit up, bright and big against the dark sky. Firing out from the roof of the long shed, which spanned the roadway, were what seemed like hundreds of spotlights, crisscrossing back and forth across our car as we approached.

Guards at the checkpoint stopped the car and ordered us to get out. We girls were separated from our parents and taken inside the elongated shed to a small room. It seemed to me as if we stood there huddled together and alone for hours. When we were finally led back outside, our parents were standing rigidly beside the car. Guards searched it from top to bottom. Our suitcases were piled up on the sidewalk and the doors of the car stood open, along with the roof of the trunk. A guard stood leaning over the trunk, his body half inside the depth of the car and his hands reaching down and pushing back into the empty spaces. Another guard circled the car with a mirror on wheels that allowed him to search underneath, while another perched in the front seat of the car and reached into the back, peeling back the seating to peer beneath the cushions. The guards even opened wide the hood of the car to stare deep into its guts.

"What are they looking for?" I asked.

"Shhh!" My mother shook her head, her lips pursed tightly together. One of the guards turned to look at me. His face was impassive, his eyes cold and his mouth a straight line of disapproval. When the search of the car was over, we were given back our passports, allowed to get in our car, and told to drive on to the other side. We passed through the no-man's-land between East and West, a stretch of fifty yards of asphalt glittering under the passing spotlights. Darkness reached in from either side of the traverse, and the gates of West Berlin beckoned before us. My father finally answered my question.

"They were looking for people in our car, seeing if we were carrying any relatives to the West."

"And if they found someone?" I asked.

"They would be taken away, maybe killed." My father was angry, looking back through the rearview mirror. He was not looking at us girls in the backseat. He was looking at the guards we'd left behind.

I saw my mother shoot my father a warning look, but he went on. "People die every day trying to leave, trying to get to the West. Do you understand?"

"Yes," Anne-Marie answered for all of us. She reached for my hand and squeezed.

One week later we flew home to Chicago. In my excitement to be home, I left *Harriet the Spy*, my notebook, and Piglet in the taxicab. My parents tried to track down the cab but without any luck. For weeks I had trouble sleeping. I woke up from nightmares I couldn't remember, crying and shaking. My mother bought me a new copy of *Harriet the Spy*, and a family friend sewed me a new Piglet. I bought myself a clean notebook and started in writing all over again. I wrote about Harriet, about Carol and about my grandmother, about my relatives in Poland and the terrors of Checkpoint Charlie. I wrote a poem about Anne-Marie and her hand coming for me across the lumpy mattress of my aunt's bed, and then across the backseat of our car as it carried us into the West. I don't have that notebook any longer, but I do have my second copy of *Harriet the Spy*, and I do have the stuffed pig. Comfort of the pig I outgrew—comfort of the book, never.

I needed comfort now. I needed hope. Hope that when life turns on you for the worst, it will turn back again, for the good. We girls had been protected for so long from misfortune. But then everything changed. My sister, the one with the reaching hand, was dead. Life had unleashed its unfairness, its random dispersal of pain, its uncaring lynching of certainty. I had tried running, but now I would try reading. I would trust in Connolly's promise that "words are alive, and literature becomes an escape, not from, but into living."

My book reading would be a discipline. I knew there would be pleasure in my reading, but I needed to hold myself to a schedule as well. Without a commitment, the rest of life could creep in and steal time away, and I wouldn't read as much as I wanted to or needed to. I couldn't have my escape if I didn't make books my priority. There is always dust to sweep and laundry to fold; there is always milk to buy and dinner to cook and dishes to wash. But none of that could get in my way for one year. I was allowing myself one year to not run, not plan, not provide. A year of nots: not worry, not control, not make money. Sure, our family could use another income, but we'd gotten by for so long on just one salary, we could do it for one more year. We would lay off the extras and find enough in what we had already.

I planned to begin my book-a-day project on my forty-sixth birthday. I would read my first book that day, and the next day I would write my first review. The rules for my year were simple: no author could be read more than once; I couldn't re-read any books I'd already read; and I had to write about every book I read. I would read new books and new authors, and read old books from favorite writers. I wouldn't read *War and Peace*, but I could read Tolstoy's last novel, *The Forged Coupon*. All the books would be ones I would have shared with Anne-Marie if I could have, ones we would have talked about, argued over, and some we would have agreed upon.

The summer before I turned forty-six, I had put together

a Web site for book exchanges—allowing people who needed books to connect with people who wanted to give their old books away—and I decided to use that Web site as a place where I'd record my year of reading a book a day. It was already called Read All Day, a premonition of my life to come. Perfect. Anyone who has kids in school knows how hyped-up librarians and teachers are about getting kids to read every single day. I agreed with the hype, but why not push reading for adults too? Why not foster daily reading in adults? My year of intense reading would be my own project of escape, but my site would also be a place for nudging along other adults in their reading. The motto of the Read All Day Web site was "Great Good Comes from Reading Great Books." My year could prove its truth.

I set myself up in a room downstairs, off the kitchen. It had a piano in it and George's tuba, along with a few discarded recorders and plenty of old music books. The room had two bookshelves, and I cleared away space for the books I'd be getting from the library, from bookstores, and from family. I dragged a paint-stained wooden desk—stolen from the playroom—and placed on top of it the computer abandoned to me by Meredith, my stepdaughter, when she'd upgraded to a laptop. There was one big chair in the room, and I pondered its fate.

The chair looked older than it was, but then it had been through a lot in the thirteen years we'd owned it. Jack had brought it home a few days before Michael was born. At the time, it was the most elegant piece of furniture in our apartment, glorious with its ivory white raised upholstery, ridged mahogany legs, amply stuffed arms, and gracefully curved back. But white? With our Magic Marker–equipped one-year-old on the loose and a baby on the way, it wouldn't remain white for long. And I knew from past experience that there would be more than just juice boxes leaking on the furniture with a new baby to be fed.

The chair stayed in our apartment—as it was purchased on sale, there was no returning it—but it did not stay white for long. Patches began to appear, with a rainbow of colors, purple (wine), brown (coffee), pink (Magic Marker), blue (bubble gum ice cream), and yellow (milk). By the time we came to child number three, the chair was so stained it looked like a world map. But it was still sturdy and very comfortable, the arms still amply stuffed and providing a good cushion for rocketing children. We had the chair reupholstered in a very tough fabric, muted purple with a pattern of flowers and vines, and invincible against stains.

As invincible as the chair was against stains, it was powerless against cats. Or one cat, in particular. Milo had been brought home from the shelter as a gift for Michael. He was a black-and-white longhair. Sweet in disposition, he meowed rarely and never scratched the furniture. But he did have one fault. Every once in a while he would pee, just a tiny, little bit, on the purple chair. It was as if he were marking the chair as his beloved chair and his alone. His marking worked. The odor of cat pee is daunting to the average nose-owning human, and no one could sit there for longer than a minute or two before hightailing it out of the chair. My husband wanted to dump the chair after smelling the ablutions of Milo's love, but I revolted. It was too good a chair, and I had by now too many memories associated with it. Meredith read to Peter snuggled up in that chair, Michael's birth announcement photo had been shot there, and the chair had been George's favorite nursing spot. Peter used it as a prop in his one-act plays involving kings and queens. Although it smelled, it was still regal.

I placed the chair in the farthest corner of the house and sprayed it daily with a magical elixir that managed to dull the odor to only mildly repulsive. The spray also worked to repel all future dousing by Milo. He never sat in or marked the chair again. Over the years the odor faded, and by now the chair had no real odor, only an occasional disagreeable whiff. It was still very sturdy and even more comfortable. The purple chair would be my dedicated reading chair.

I was ready—ready to sit down in my purple chair and read. For years, books had offered to me a window into how other people deal with life, its sorrows and joys and monotonies and frustrations. I would look there again for empathy, guidance, fellowship, and experience. Books would give me all that, and more. After three years of carrying the truth of my sister's death around with me, I knew I would never be relieved of my sorrow. I was not hoping for relief. I was hoping for answers. I was trusting in books to answer the relentless question of why I deserved to live. And of how I should live. My year of reading would be my escape back into life.

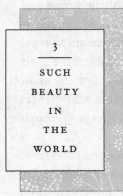

3

SUCH
BEAUTY
IN
THE
WORLD

*Thinking back on it, this evening, with my heart
and my stomach all like jelly, I have finally
concluded, maybe that's what life is about: there
is a lot of despair, but also the odd moment of
beauty, where time is no longer the same . . .
an always within never.*

MURIEL BARBERY,
The Elegance of the Hedgehog

I STARTED READING *THE ELEGANCE OF THE HEDGEHOG* BY
Muriel Barbery on the train ride into New York City on the
day of my forty-sixth birthday. The day had started with
breakfast served up alongside kisses and hugs, envelopes and
homemade cards waiting to the side. There was the usual card
from my son Michael with its accurately numbered candles on
the cake, each drawn in with its own flame. This was a cake to
be wary of: so many candles, so much fire. There was a card
from the cats, signed "from the cats" by Jack. We've always
had cats but Jack never knows their names.

I opened the envelopes that had come in through the mail
over the last few days. There was a card from my parents and
one from Jack's parents, with the yearly cash enclosed. With
fifty-plus children, grandchildren, great-grandchildren, and
daughters- and sons-in-law, Jack's parents could go broke
with birthday-card cash, but until they did, the gift was always
there.

There was a final pile of cards for me to read, the slew of
Hallmark mush that my husband is a sucker for and that I have
come to look forward to. Tears and smiles along with our

peanut-butter toast and coffee. I was grateful to be loved. I knew that most days I took the love for granted, just like I had taken life for granted, and this day I wanted to be different. I would begin my year of reading with gratitude. Gratitude for having all these lives and this love around me. Gratitude for living on into my forty-sixth year.

I smiled and cried some more when Natasha called to wish me a happy day. After breakfast I answered e-mails wishing me joy for the coming year. Only a few people knew of my plan to read a book every day for a year, and no one mentioned it. Everyone was sure I would have to drop out of the planned year of reading, and no one wanted to make me feel embarrassed if I did. They figured my obligations at school or the kids getting sick or holidays and vacations would force me to miss a day here or there. They thought I would end up scaling back, reading one or two books a week. But I knew I would stick with my books project. I was ready for the discipline. The plan could work around school hours and the driving, cleaning, cooking, and grocery shopping, and still meet its goals of escape, learning, pleasure. I was aching for that, needing that comfort of reading and anticipating the pleasure of sitting down in my purple chair with a book and calling it work. By giving it the name of work, I sanctified it.

Reading had always been a favorite thing to do, but now it would become a worthy endeavor. I could excuse myself from coffees, PTA meetings, and exercise by having work to do. Most everyone thought my project was crazy, but that didn't matter, not too much anyway. It was what I needed. I knew I was lucky to have the time and support to do this, and I wouldn't waste either. Once I'd made the decision to take on my book-a-day year, I did not question the commitment or the pleasure ahead. I made a plan, and then I stopped debating the pluses or minuses. I would take the time I could have spent debating my choice and instead throw myself into carrying it out.

When Jack and I talked about getting married, and then when we thought about having kids, I had been the same way. I made my choice and followed through with actions taken full force ahead, body and soul. Jack was the one, and I married him, for better and forget the worse. Four kids I wanted, and I had them one after the other, sticking my legs up into the air after sex to ensure fertilization and then, nine months later, using those legs as an anchor during delivery.

Now I had committed to reading a book a day. Not quite like marriage or motherhood but a commitment, nevertheless.

Reading *The Elegance of the Hedgehog* on the train was tough going at first. The first forty or so pages of the novel have lots of obscure references thrown in here and there about philosophy and music, movies and art. But I soon fell in love with the two narrators, Paloma and Renée. Paloma is twelve years old and mired in existential angst. She hides both her intelligence and her despair behind a caustic wit and manga novels. She's certain that there is no purpose or meaning to life, and she vows to kill herself on her thirteenth birthday. Wow and whoa: this kid cannot be serious. But I feared that she was.

Renée, the concierge of the high-toned building where Paloma lives, hides behind the facade of a dull, slow-witted working-class drone so that she can be invisible to the people around her. She wants to be left in peace to secretly enjoy the pleasure and comfort that books, music, art, and good food bring to her. I knew I had found a kindred spirit in Renée when I read her thoughts on books: "When something is bothering me, I seek refuge. No need to travel far; a trip to the realm of literary memory will suffice. For where can one find more noble distraction, more entertaining company, more delightful enchantment, than in literature?" Right on.

By the time my train hit New York City, I was hooked on *The Elegance of the Hedgehog.* I put it away long enough to have a birthday lunch with Jack and my parents. We sat on a balcony overlooking the Main Concourse at Grand Central and drank champagne. As we ate our meal, I told them about how it had been Anne-Marie who'd first pointed out Grand Central's magnificent ceiling to me, its golden constellations set into the barrel ceiling of the huge space. I had read about the ceiling in Mark Helprin's mythical *Winter's Tale* (a must read, if only for the ceiling description and the scene of a mighty mother skating triumphantly down the frozen Hudson River, baby on her back), but that was after Anne-Marie first showed it to me. The stars and figures were hard to make out in those days before its restoration, but under Anne-Marie's pointing finger, I gaped at the scope of the constellations. Anne-Marie had given architectural tours of New York City as a graduate student at NYU's Institute of Fine Arts, and she knew her stuff.

The ceiling in Grand Central is fascinating for a lot of reasons, but what most people don't realize is that the entire night sky is presented backward. The artist Paul César Helleu based his sky on a medieval manuscript that represented a God's-eye view of the universe, seen from above the stars rather than from below. "Or else Helleu just made a huge mistake and tried to explain it away by using the medieval excuse," Anne-Marie explained. I could tell she thought he'd been a lazy scholar and made the huge mistake. Careful as she was in her own work, there was no question the ceiling would have been perfect under her direction.

Hopelessly late for the high school drop-off, I hopped back on the train after lunch to make it home in time for the middle school bus. I continued reading on the train, any potential sleepiness brought on by the several glasses of champagne beaten back by the story: I read with eyes wide open. Barely glancing up at the ticket collector, I mumbled, "Thanks" and thumbed on through the pages. A new tenant moves into the building where Paloma and Renée live. He befriends the two of them, and the gentle force of Kakuro's friendship coaxes Paloma, and then Renée, out of hiding. They begin to reveal their inner selves and to find in each other understanding and appreciation. Together, the three of them, Kakuro, Paloma, and Renée, recognize the infinite possibilities of surprise that life offers. Neither people nor life is so predictable after all.

I arrived home in time to dish out after-school snacks. Peanut butter on crackers, apple slices, apple juice. Chocolates given to me by my mother, shared now with the boys. More birthday kisses, and then I took myself away. I planted myself in my purple chair. I had just a few more chapters to go in *The Elegance of the Hedgehog*.

Would Paloma stop fearing her future? Would Renée stop fearing her past? The last pages of the book were brilliant with wisdom. Each moment caught in a lifetime of experience can be brought forward. Sustenance in the here and now is found in the past. Good things have happened before and will happen again. Moments of beauty and light and happiness live forever. Paloma commits herself to finding those "moments of always within never" as a reason to live. She is anticipating moments of beauty because she knows they will come. The proof is in the moments she has already experienced. I could find those "moments of always within never" as a comfort to my pain, and as a promise for my future. I remembered what I had forgotten in my years of sorrow after Anne-Marie died: that I would always have my memories of Anne-Marie to sustain me.

I walked out into the kitchen, slammed the book down on the counter, and said to my kids, "This is going to be a great year."

The Elegance of the Hedgehog reminded me, bone and blood, heart and soul, of Anne-Marie. It was as if I could hear her saying to me, "Yes, Nina, life is hard, unfair, painful. But life is also guaranteed—one hundred percent, no doubt, no question—to offer unexpected and sudden moments of beauty, joy, love, acceptance, euphoria." The good stuff. It is our ability to recognize and then hold on to the moments of good stuff that allows us to survive, even thrive. And when we can share the beauty, hope is restored.

People often talk about the importance of living in the here and now, and express envy at how children enjoy their moments of pleasure without dwelling on the past or worrying about the future. Fine, agreed. But it is experience—a life lived—that allows us to recall moments of happiness and feel happy again. It is our ability to relive a moment that gives us strength. Our survival as a species is linked to this ability to remember (which berries not to eat; to stay away from the big toothy animals; to huddle close to fire but not touch it). But survival of our inner selves also depends upon memories. Why else do we have such acute noses? I smell an evergreen and swoon with delight. Why? Because of the many pleasant hours passed at the foot of a Christmas tree. And the smell of popcorn is so seductive because of the movies I've enjoyed while eating it. The taste of a good green olive makes me hungry, because an olive or two have accompanied so many delicious meals and flowing wines.

I stood in my kitchen and looked at my children, my birthday cards set out in a standing row, the school artwork on the walls, and the last zinnias of the year picked and stuffed into a pitcher. Past and present melded together. Cards the same as every year and new cards; artwork from when my oldest was still in kindergarten and his latest piece from ninth grade, alongside paintings, masks, and prints made by his brothers over the years; zinnias planted in the spring and now picked for our pleasure in the fall. Past and present together offer hope for the future. Maybe it was my past and present that would provide the glue for the two parts of me, the part that couldn't leave Anne-Marie's hospital room and the part that couldn't get away fast enough. With books by my side, and my past and my present, all together, I would move into a future. Books, past, and present pushing me up and offering hope from what can be remembered. Offering warning of what should not be forgotten. Tamping back the blood from the harsh cuts of living.

Could memories of times when I was filled with peace, or overflowing with love, or resplendent in gratitude sustain me through the horror of losing my sister? Renée demonstrated to Paloma—and to me—that if we are mindful enough to grasp the beauty of such moments, we can hang on to those moments forever. Kakuro showed both of them—and me—that such moments are best shared, either in the moment or in memory. And Paloma showed Renée—and me—how life's possibilities, future memories to find and grasp, can chisel away at imprisoning sorrow.

I remembered then how entwined memory had come to me before and offered comfort. I spent my junior year of college abroad in Barcelona. One rainy afternoon a few months after I'd settled into life there, I went by myself to the Museu d'Art Modern in the Parc de la Ciutadella. The museum was empty, owing to the weather and the season (not a hot time for tourists), and I took my time walking from room to room. I was thinking about a boy I'd just broken up with. Nico was a sweet boy with a great motorcycle and good looks but not much else. There was no point to my relationship with him, and yet he had been fun to be with. He helped keep my homesickness at bay, and he showed me parts of Barcelona I wouldn't have found on my own. I had suspected that my entertainment value as the American girl was fading, especially given my reluctance to do more than hold his waist as we weaved in and out of traffic on his motorcycle. We kissed and hugged during our nights out together, but I resisted anything further. I didn't want to fulfill the reputation of the easy American, and I suspected there was an old girlfriend waiting patiently for him every evening after he dropped me off.

The evening before my solo trip to the museum, Nico had taken me for a ride on his motorcycle north of Barcelona along the coast. We arrived finally at a long pier, busy with other motorcycles moving slowly up and down its long, wide boards leading out into the sea. We rode almost to the end of the pier. We stopped, and I looked out across the black expanse of water.

A shift in clouds let the moon come through. Suddenly the water was alive, glittering and sparkling with a long, undulating ribbon of moonbeam. I can remember still how cold it was that evening, the salty smell of the air, the low hum of other couples as they rolled up and down the pier, and the mesmerizing play of moonlight over the water. Nico tried to get me started on a session of kissing and groping, but I pulled away, climbing off the bike to get closer to the sea. This view was what I wanted; I had never seen anything like it. The water was exploding with lights, like firecrackers in the sky, the light of the moon reflecting and multiplying across the waves. I did not want to leave. I wanted to stay out on that pier until the moonlight settled down. I wanted to be there when the sun came up and a different light, the warming glow of day, came over the water. But Nico was insistent that he had to get back to the city. I climbed onto the motorcycle, and we rode off. We both knew our relationship was over.

As I walked through the museum the next day, I came upon a painting of a sunrise. It was not the sunrise I'd wanted the night before, orange and pink over a long expanse of water. But it was beautiful. The painting was a large landscape of dawn rising over a dark hillside. In one corner of the painting, a hermit is coming out of his cave in the hill. He has raised his eyes and pushed back the cowl of his robe to look out over the countryside. Apricot orange lines of sunrise glow against a pale gray background, lighting up the sky beyond the hermit's darkened burrow. The grass along the edge of his cave looks frosted with icy dew, but beyond, on the hillside, small flowers unfurl under the sun's first light. I don't remember if birds were painted into the picture, but I do remember hearing them. I stood for almost one hour in front of that painting. I heard the birds and I felt the thawing wind of spring, the precious beat of living, the gratitude for another day granted.

As I stood there, memories of mornings I'd woken early and gone out into a day just starting (the orange-and-pink-stained sky, the damp on the ground and the sharpness in the air, the birds) entwined with the experience of seeing this painting now before me. Layers of memories formed a cocoon around me: the night before on the pier anticipating a dawn, this painting, mornings in my past. Layers of time to be stored and later savored. The memories invoked by that painting, feeling the spring wind and understanding the hermit's gratitude, smelling the flowers and sensing the icy dew, were memories that, when brought back, sustained and comforted me that cold, wet day in Barcelona. I knew, standing there, looking at the hermit in his hillside idyll, that I would not be lonely in Barcelona. I would awake to mornings and find the same joy shown in this painting. I could go out from this museum and call on my memory of that painting, and of the memories invoked by that painting, and I would feel good. And the memory of the evening before, the ride out to the end of a pier, arms wrapped around a boy I'd never see again, the cold and the salt and then the sudden flashing of moonlight across the water: I would hold on to that memory as well. And over the years, I have.

I hold on to many memories. When my oldest son was just a few months old, I took him out onto the Great Lawn of Central Park. This was in the years before the makeover of the Great Lawn. Now it is a plush stretch of the finest Kentucky grass, interspersed with raked-sand ball fields and cared for by an army of workers (and they are militant). The Great Lawn today is protected by a high fence that stretches around its entire perimeter. The few gates allowing entrance are closed on days when rain has left the ground wet and vulnerable, and on other days for seemingly no reason at all. But that fall, when Peter was a baby, the Great Lawn was a dusty, potholed round of patchy grass and dirt, ringed not by a prohibiting fence but by trees in full autumn blaze. The air was sharp and cold, and dusk was not far off. I sat down on a mound of dirt, took Peter onto my lap, and contemplated what this moment meant. Our trip across uneven ground, amid the bitten-off cold and the smell of pounded earth like leather, the last light of day exploding against fall's leaves like rust on the circle of trees: I knew I would never forget this moment shared with my son. But would he remember? Years ahead, falls ahead, would his senses tense to the same pitch of cold, light, and smell, and would he know the same exhilaration of waiting for the end of day? I wanted him to feel me then as he did now in my lap, my love a flicker of recognition felt in a future where I might be far away, a bit of warmth against the cold falling fast.

It is a gift we humans have, to hold on to beauty felt in a moment for a lifetime. Suddenly beauty comes to us, and gratefully we take it. We may not be able to recite time and place, but the memories can come flooding back, felt full force without warning or brought on purposefully by a triggering event. The smell of pinecones, the whiff of popcorn, the taste of a cold beer, or the bite of mint: a jumble of feelings, and then a sudden clarity of beauty or joy or sadness. Beauty is in the moments that endure, the moments that enliven us again and again. We stand on memory's sturdy pilings. We thrive on the nourishment provided by the past.

A few weeks before Anne-Marie died, she went for a walk in the Conservatory Garden in Central Park in New York City. The Conservatory Garden is an enclosed garden, the only enclosure in Central Park other than the fenced croquet course by Sheep Meadow, Sheep Meadow itself, and now the Great Lawn. But in contrast to the plain fences of the croquet course, meadow, and lawn, the Conservatory Garden is enclosed by beauty, by overgrown bushes and fawning trees and mossy stone walls and ornate iron gates. The garden is a three-part symphony of color and sculpture, of fountains and benches and shaded alleys and sunny corners. In the springtime ten thousand tulip bulbs bloom, and in the summer riots of every kind of flower, vine, bush, and grass flourish. In the fall, thousands of mums burst forth in shades of purple, cream, pink, and orange. Winter is marked by quiet, by stark branches of trees etched against the sky and stilled and emptied fountains.

The day that Anne-Marie went out for a walk was a sunny day in April. Her last April. In the garden, the green foliage of the peonies and iris gave background to purple and white crocuses, yellow and cream and orange narcissus, and the blues of scilla and hyacinth. Anne-Marie walked leaning heavily on Marvin, but she was glad to be outside. That morning they had received a phone call. A colleague had committed suicide, a young man who had lost all hope and killed himself. Walking through the garden, Anne-Marie and Marvin talked about the death. Anne-Marie looked around her at the spring flowers and up at the blue sky shining through the flowering apple trees preening overhead. As ill as she was, and as certain as she was that her own death would come sooner rather than later, she turned to Marvin and said she could not understand the impulse to suicide, the complete enveloping of gloom that would allow someone to take his own life: "For who can end in despair when there is such beauty in the world?"

She was right. There is always an answer to despair, and that is the promise of beauty waiting in the future. I know it is coming because I have seen and felt beauty in the past. Stacks of apricots in Rome; raccoon footprints in snow; piles of oyster shells bleached white over winter; lime green leaves of spring; burnt orange leaves of fall; Vermeer's *Young Woman with a Water Pitcher*; the old stone walls of Connecticut winding around my yard; Venice at dusk, rose-colored from sky and sea: memories of beauty, sometimes experienced alone and sometimes shared.

Colum McCann, author of *Let the Great World Spin*, talks about a visit he made to London when he was just a boy. He went there from Dublin to visit his dying grandfather. While in London, his father took him out for a hamburger, and when the waitress, Irish herself, heard why the young boy had come to London, she touched his cheek and brought him an ice-cream sundae. He has remembered that waitress his whole life. Those moments of her kindness and sympathy were exactly the kind of chance connections that led McCann to write the magnificent *Let the Great World Spin*. Those moments are the moments that can be brought forward through time to sustain hope. Those moments can reignite belief that the world can be a kind and forgiving place. Those moments are beauty.

In *Nothing to Be Frightened Of*, Julian Barnes talks about how in remembering such moments of beauty, he allows himself to expect them to come again. Giving up on life is unimaginable for Barnes because there is always the "promise of a new novel or a new friend (or an old novel or an old friend), or a football match on television." I love that line for how Barnes revels in the quiet and simple joys as being enough reason to live. I will never again have the joy of holding my newborn in my arms—those days are over for me—but the pleasures of a book or a painting or a walk in the park are both in my past, and sure to come in my future.

Looking backward in order to move forward. In her poem "Stepping Backward," Adrienne Rich recommends the backward glance for gaining fuller perspective: "We live by inches and only sometimes see the full dimension." Looking backward allows me to see the entirety of my present life, of what it took to get me to where I am, and of what I want to have in the life still ahead of me. The big picture, the great perspective. I understand what is important by looking back to see what I remember.

Later in my year of reading, I would again come across the admonition to look backward, for "such glances always make us wiser." The line was in the stories collected in Nathaniel Hawthorne's *Twice-Told Tales*. The copy I had was an old one, printed in 1890. Someone before me had underlined the line, and it struck me also. Such glances behind do keep one moving ahead with a bit of wisdom. And so I would go on with my year: present reading, past memories, future wisdom.

I understood why I was where I was now, with a whole year of new books stretching out before me. I was here to read, as planned. But it was also necessary for me to go back, to my past. *The Elegance of the Hedgehog* gave me the first hint that my plan for a year of reading would change. My plan would evolve as the year progressed, and I couldn't know how. My year of escape would be something very different from what I had expected. Comfort, yes; pleasure, of course. But now I also had a mandate to go backward and recover memories. And an even greater mandate: to share what I found in books, intertwined with my memories. I would write about what I read not only as my own recording of an endeavor but to share with whoever stopped by my Read All Day Web site the magic of the books I was sinking down into. I would find "the odd moment of beauty," and the "always within never." I would hold those moments tightly while also passing them on. What else would change in my plan of reading and writing? I could not even guess. My year of magical reading was on.

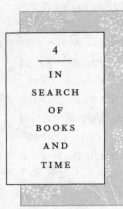

"What did I ever give her?"
"The happiness of giving."

EDITH WHARTON,
The Touchstone

I WENT TO THE LIBRARY IN EARLY NOVEMBER, IN SEARCH of books. Adding a new method to my lifelong formula for library search and seizure, I found an armload for my second week of reading. The new method involved the usual browsing of the stacks and selecting anything with a good title, but I added the twist of reaching only for those books with a width of one inch. A one-inch thickness in a hardcover book of average height (nine to ten inches) generally translates to a total page count of about 250 to 300 pages. Because I read about seventy pages an hour, I can read a three-hundred-page book in just over four hours. Reviewing that book would take more time. Just a few days' experience of writing reviews had shown me that a review had no definite time allotment. It could take me half an hour or five hours, depending on how much the book meant to me and how easy or hard it was for me to translate what the book meant into words on my computer screen. I averaged out the reviewing time to about two hours and planned accordingly.

Six hours to read and write equaled the six hours I had more or less to myself every day, at least during the week. Weekends were unpredictable, but I could stake a claim to four hours each morning, especially if I got up early. I planned out my year: if I spent two hours writing and posting a review, I would have no problem finishing up the daily book by the time school-day buses rolled in (and the corresponding waves of snacks, homework, activities, and meltdowns or euphoria that had to be shared). I would be able to plan and cook dinner (not well, but no worse than before my book-a-day year started); I could keep laundry under control (clean underwear in every drawer); and summary cleaning would get done (and I mean summary: crumbs off counters, dishes in dishwasher, kitty litter filtered and tossed). Weekends I would have to do some reading at night, but that was fine—I could swing it by ordering in pizza and relying on Jack for at least one good dinner. I would be able to write my reviews, enjoy my books, and be there for my family as greeter, driver, food shopper and server, cleaner, cook, friend, counselor, disciplinarian, lover (to my husband, on occasion, and not often enough), and overall, overlord of the manse.

And so there I was, in the library cruising the stacks, look-ing for the right width and the good titles, the interesting au-thors, new ones and some old ones. I picked up books and put them back again. I found eight or so that I wanted to read. I checked them out and brought them home to sit on a shelf next to books I'd been given for my birthday. What in years past would have been a month or two of reading material now equaled less than two weeks of reading. A shiver of excitement passed through me. I could do this! I felt as if I'd won the lot-tery and played the best trick ever, all rolled up in one great feeling of complete gratitude. Life was good.

I skimmed the titles waiting on the shelf. My finger stopped on *Death with Interruptions* by José Saramago. Saramago, a

Portuguese writer, won the Nobel Prize for Literature in 1998. I loved his books *Blindness* (made into a movie with Julianne Moore, Mark Ruffalo, and Danny Glover) and *The Cave*. *Death with Interruptions* was his latest, found on the new-releases shelf at the library. It was due back within three days. No problem: I would read it today, review it tomorrow, and return it over the weekend.

I took the book and walked into the kitchen to make myself some lunch. I was getting started late today—what with my trip to the library—but *Death with Interruptions* is a book of less than 300 pages, and I trusted Saramago to make the pages fly.

The book begins with the sentence: "The following day, no one died." And so I found myself in a country where no one dies. Sounded good to me. Thirty-five minutes, forty-three pages, and one lunch later, the phone rang. Caller ID showed it was a Westport Public Schools phone number. I could not ignore this call. I put my pencil in the book to mark the page and clicked the talk button on my phone.

"Hello, Nina. It's Sandra over at Kings Highway. Martin has been in twice already today complaining of a bad tummy, and now he's thrown up." Sandra was the school nurse and a very good assessor of kids' maladies, both of the mind and body. This time the assessment and diagnosis seemed easy enough. Martin had to come home.

"Is he okay?"

Sandra understood what I meant. Were there tears? "No, he's fine, just wants his mom and a bed with a bucket beside it."

"Is there a bug going around?"

"Yes, and it's a bad one, only twenty-four hours but nothing pretty."

"I'll come get him. Be there in about ten minutes."

It was nine thirty at night before I got back to *Death with*

Interruptions. Martin needed hovering over and dinner needed cooking and boys needed nudging into bed. Now I had two and a half hours left until midnight and almost two hundred pages still to read. I sank into the purple chair and into the book. I could feel the pull of the words drawing me in, holding me tight in anticipation and pleasure. Luckily for me, the best part of the book—and all of this book is so good—is in its final chapters. I got to them at eleven o'clock, and any weariness that had started creeping in vanished. I had no trouble staying awake through death's attempted seduction of the young man she has fallen in love with and her final surrender to love. Love overcoming death—yes!

Midnight came. The book was finished, and I gave a sigh of satisfaction. It was a great read, and it would be an interesting one to write about. No problem that I was up so late. The weekend had officially started, and I could sleep in tomorrow. I set the alarm beside my bed for seven (one whole extra hour of sleep!) and turned out the light.

The next day's offering of nonstop Saturday cartoons made it easy to keep Martin lying down, resting in front of the television. The hard part was keeping him apart from his brothers, but I had to do it. I didn't want the bug spreading through the family. Waving the (empty) blue bucket/family vomitorium over my head, I warned the older brothers about the illness, and told them Martin had to stay segregated on his own couch, untouched and unbothered. The sight of that waving bucket was enough of a deterrent, and when Jack offered to take the older boys out for pancakes, I was left alone in the house. With a puking child.

I wrote my review in bits and pieces, hustling back and forth between the bathtub, where I washed out Martin's bucket again and again, and the poor kid himself, shivering and pale. He looked so small lying on the huge green couch, his body hidden under the fleece blanket, one skinny arm reaching out to hold on to the bucket. I sat beside him, stroking his hair back from his face, feeling his forehead for warmth. No fever. I raced back to the computer and hassled with the review. Back to Martin and the bucket. Back to the computer to finally post the review.

That afternoon Martin slept the hours away, and I stayed close, reading. I chose *The Touchstone* by Edith Wharton, a short book, and felt myself relaxing, sinking into the couch beside Martin while I read. By dinnertime Martin was better, charging around after his brothers and hollering for food. Jack fixed up some pasta, and I read on in *The Touchstone*.

The Touchstone is about morality and identity, as are all of Wharton's books. She is the master of pulling back the curtains of propriety and custom to reveal the duality of life, the struggle between publicly identifying—"finding"—oneself and deliberately hiding what is private or shameful in an effort to bolster respectability, wealth, and, most important, security. Wharton enveloped her insights on human nature within page-turning plots of love, intrigue, and betrayal. *The Touchstone* is perfect storytelling and was a quick and good read.

I finished the book easily by dinnertime, in turn laughing at Wharton's hilarious passages about wedded bliss ("The tiny lawn was smooth as a shaven cheek, and a crimson ramble mounted to the nursery window of a baby who never cried") and shaking at her insight into the role of beneficence, where "the happiness of giving" offers satisfaction to both parties, the one in need and the one bestowing what is needed. I promised myself that the evening would be reserved for Jack, my kind and giving husband, who had taken care of three meals to allow me all the time I needed to both read my book and coddle a sick child. Saturday night, book finished, boys in bed, and inspired by Wharton, I went to give Jack my own overdue messages of love and marriage. But he was asleep on the couch, and I soon joined him, passed out on the other couch, television on but unwatched. The messages would have to wait.

Monday morning, Martin was completely recovered. I had four boys getting on buses, with only moderate grumbling and no last-minute dashes for anything. I showered and dressed, poured a fresh cup of coffee, and sat down in front of my computer, ready to write up a quick review of *Silks*, the new Dick Francis mystery I'd read on Sunday. Sundays were my mystery days, the day I allowed myself candy and soda in the form of fast-paced, gripping novels of detection, sleuthing, and resolution.

Silks had been great fun to read, but the review was harder to write than I had anticipated. How to convey the sheer entertainment value of a good Francis, while also acknowledging its formulaic unfolding? I struggled through for more than two hours and then sat back to do a spell-check. The phone rang, and in my urgency to see if another stomach bug had come to plague me, I hit the wrong button on my computer. When I came back from a call asking about my satisfaction with my cable service (Damn! I reminded myself to look at the caller ID number every time), I found an empty screen before me—total erasure of what I had spent the morning writing.

By the time I stopped yelling like an idiot at the blank screen and pounded out another review, it was lunchtime. I wasn't hungry. I was frustrated. Forget lunch, forget the laundry I'd planned on getting started this morning, forget my plan to fumigate the big green couch/sickbed. I had to start reading my book of the day, and I had to start now. I grabbed *The Master of Petersburg* by J. M. Coetzee off the shelf, shoved myself down into my purple chair, and began to read. In what seemed like only minutes, the back door swung open. The shouts of returning boys echoed through the house.

Another night up until midnight. Real life had kept me from the book all afternoon. I thought of Edith Wharton's "happiness of giving" as I drove boys here and there, did a slapdash grocery run (bread, bananas, milk, orange juice—my daily mantra of what we always seem to need more of), scooted to the train to pick up Jack, and pushed loads of laundry through the washer. Everyone wanted dinner—surprise! I overcooked some chicken cutlets and tossed a premade salad. I cleaned up from dinner, folded laundry, and began straightening up the house and getting kids ready for bed. When I finally could sit down again with Coetzee and Dostoyevsky, it was ten o'clock. I was tired, bone-tired. I was downstairs alone, while my husband slept alone upstairs: messages of love out the window, we'd have to try again tomorrow.

The happiness I got from giving to family was getting all mixed up with my scheduling. I could schedule reading, writing, cooking, and cleaning. But how to schedule caring and loving? The "happiness in giving" would have to come the other way now, as boys and husband worked to make time and space for me and my books. A book a day? For one year? I would need all the time and space—and love—they could give me. And I promised to give back all the happiness I found.

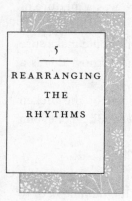

5

—

REARRANGING
THE
RHYTHMS

The weird world rolls on.

PAUL AUSTER,
quoting Rose Hawthorne, *Man in the Dark*

THE NEXT EVENING AT DINNER I ANNOUNCED A NEW HOUSE-
hold policy. I'd put together a cleanup schedule. The two older
boys were on duty cleaning up after dinner, two days on and
two days off, and I would clean up on weekends. The younger
boys were responsible for setting and clearing the table on al-
ternate days. The boys would also help with laundry, bringing
dirty clothes to the laundry room and putting away cleaned
clothes.

"Your allowance will go up," I promised.

"But you never remember to pay us," Michael said.

"You never remember to ask me," I answered, while making a note in my brain to pay allowance every week, without
fail.

After dinner, George approached me with a book in his
hand.

"I really want you to read this book, Mom. I think you
would like it."

I took the book from him. *Watership Down* by Richard Adams. I knew it was one of George's favorites. I opened it up,
turned to the last page. The book was almost five hundred

pages long. I looked up at George. His face was a mixture of challenge and supplication.

"If you're going to read a book a day, you should make sure the books are good ones," he offered, "and I know this is a good book. I want you to read it."

I nodded. "Of course I will." I placed it down on the kitchen counter, on top of other waiting books. "*That* will be one long day of reading," I said.

"You're not going to read it tomorrow?" he asked.

"No, but soon, I promise."

George frowned, and I groaned inside. It would be hard to find a day with enough time in it for such a long book. But how could I say no to one of my boys?

According to my dry cleaner, I had given birth to four boys because of the dried dates I'd eaten on my wedding night. The conjugal activity I'd engaged in that same night, repeated at regular intervals in the following months and years, played only a minor role, according to Mrs. Kahng. Using photographs from her son's recent wedding, Mrs. Kahng explained to me an old Korean wedding tradition. In one photo, she is tossing chestnuts and dates at her son and new daughter-in-law, while they struggle to catch the flying foods in a cloth they hold stretched between the two of them. There is pride on Mrs. Kahng's face, glee on the groom's face, and determination on the bride's. The number of chestnuts caught is the number of girls the couple will have, and the number of dates is the number of boys.

My dry cleaner then showed me another photo, this one of the young couple clutching a colorfully wrapped package.

"The captured dates and nuts are in there," Mrs. Kahng explained. "They must eat those goodies on their wedding night, and then . . ." Nudge, nudge, wink, wink. Yes, I understood, even with no photo provided.

Peter arrived early in the marriage, born just a few months after our first wedding anniversary. Michael came two years later, George three after that, and Martin three years after George. Not exactly boom-boom-boom, but close. If I had continued having children, I am sure I would have had more boys, although I'm not sure how many chopped dates made it onto my wedding-night salad so many years ago. I wanted a big family, having grown up reading about happy times shared by siblings in books like the Bobbsey Twins series (four kids in the family), *All-of-a-Kind-Family* by Sydney Taylor (five kids), *The Saturdays* by Elizabeth Enright (four kids), and, a much-reread favorite, *Cheaper by the Dozen* by Frank Gilbreth Jr. and Ernestine Gilbreth Carey (twelve kids, of course).

I figured the number four was perfect, an even number for pairing and sharing, and no ganging-up, two on one. I would have enough time to share among four kids, and moments alone with each of them. I would be able to remember each name in the fury of yelling (I am embarrassed to admit that I have yelled out the cats' names when truly angry), and I could gather all four in my arms at one time. I stopped at four, and I was home to take care of them, one after the other and all together.

For twelve years, our time together was palmy as life with date-boys should be. The word *palmy* isn't used much anymore, but it's a good one. It derives from the benefits of dates, which come from palm trees, and means glorious, prosperous, flourishing. Four boys in tow, for years we flourished and prospered. Books were at the forefront of our activities, with regular visits to the library and to the bookstore. Books were used to soothe before bed, pacify at meals (a good book can distract a four-year-old from the fact that he is eating something green), and excite and inspire as needed. When the kids needed to run around and let off steam, I used music. The "William Tell Overture" could get us galloping through the kitchen within minutes, and Madonna and Prince were perfect for dancing on couches and tables.

Lawless games of running, screaming, tagging, and hiding prevailed when we moved out of the city and found ourselves surrounded by space, indoors and out. Swings were hung from trees, bikes and scooters of all sizes piled up, and basketballs bounded about in various stages of deflation. Jack and I veered away from video games and gaming systems. Family screen time was spent on movies and old TV shows. And we always came back to books. Our bookcases overflowed with series like the Narnia books and Lemony Snicket's Series of Unfortunate Events, and all of the Hardy Boys, along with the Zack Files, the Time Warp Trio, Captain Underpants, and, of course, Harry Potter. Every day ended with books, and most days started with them, collections of *FoxTrot*, *Calvin and Hobbes*, and the Cartoon History of the Universe read beside bowls of cereal and glasses of juice.

One of my favorite children's books is *The Seven Silly Eaters* by Mary Ann Hoberman. *The Seven Silly Eaters* is about a cello-playing, book-reading, pear-shaped, wrinkled-shirt-wearing mom who delights in her children but becomes increasingly (and hilariously) careworn as she has more and more children. The kids pile up year after year, each one a more finicky eater than the last. The dad, handsome and rugged, stays in the background of the story, planting trees and lugging groceries.

The book's illustrations of a hand-hewed house on an island

56

and filled with cats, kids, laundry, musical instruments, home-made crafts, and books, books, books were like a blueprint of my own home. Okay, we were not on an island; instead we found ourselves smack down in suburban Connecticut in a house constructed by nameless builders. But those were my kids, full of good intentions and love but also opinionated, noisy, and needy. That was my husband, handsome and supportive, willing to plant the trees but leaving all the picking to me. That was my family's laundry, in piles waiting to be folded and all over the house, on the kitchen counter, the stairs, and the coffee table in front of the television. That was my unplayed cello (substitute a piano that I've been trying to learn to play for fifteen years), and those were my bookcases filled sideways and longways with books. Page after page, and day after day, of palmy days.

The palmy days of my family fled the year my sister died. The boys were hit hard by death, one after another, over a period of just months. Three weeks after Anne-Marie died, one of my husband's sisters died. Mary had been sick for years, but I always thought she would live on and on. She was a fighter, a hell-raiser, a bargain shopper, a doughnut baker, and a dream maker who put a ten-by-ten pool in her twelve-by-twelve backyard, the neighbors be damned. The first time she met me, she warned me away from the Menz family, pronouncing "Menz" in such a way as to raise many shadows of many doubts. When she saw that I was determined to stay in the clan, Mary took me in and held me close. I became an honorary sister, and when she died, I lost another sister. The boys lost another aunt.

Just days later, a popular teacher from the middle school died. Then a local family lost their dad in a car accident. During the summer, our cat Milo disappeared while we were on vacation; in September, our other cat was hit by a car and died.

The boys cried when we buried Coco in the backyard. The tears of my children seemed inexhaustible, and I was helpless against them.

I remember that fall going out for a walk alone while the boys were at school. As I walked through the winding streets that surround my house, I slipped into a fantasy of imagining. I imagined what it would be like to walk back home again and find Anne-Marie there, waiting for me. I could actually feel the relief and the joy spilling through me as I imagined coming across the lawn and seeing her, wrapped up in a warm coat, her long, skinny legs coming out from underneath and her blond head shining in the sun. I smiled as I imagined her saying, "No, it didn't all happen, my body is here still, look, I am here." I hug her so hard, and we cry and laugh and look at each other. We look the same, me and my sister, no aging and no wear.

In my imagining, we go into the house, where I show her the books I've been reading and we wait for the kids to come home from school. "Oh, they are going to be so happy," I say as we wait. The cats are there too, alive, and purring and rubbing against our legs. They understand Anne-Marie has come back as they have come back: to return us all to the old days. Anne-Marie sits at the table, chin in her hands, elbows on the table, looking almost bored. I know that pose so well. She is not bored, but she is off in another place, thinking. The kids come home, and we are all happy.

Weeks pass, and we get used to having Anne-Marie back. Time passes on in my imagining. I take Anne-Marie for granted again, and it is wonderful. Because to take someone for granted is a luxury; to have her and not think about losing her or never seeing her again, that is a gift. But I came home from my walk and Anne-Marie was not there. I have lost, and even worse, my kids have lost, the innocence of believing no one they love will ever go away.

In *Nicholas Nickleby* by Charles Dickens, Nicholas meets the Baron of Grogzwig, who recounts memories of happiness and fun, but then says, "Alas! The high and palmy days had taken boots to themselves, and were already walking off." I could not let our palmy days walk away on the boots of death and leave us. I had to bring back joy enough to reignite belief in my children that the world is not about death and that living is not about waiting to die.

And that is why I was here, in my kitchen with a pile of waiting books on the counter, and more books waiting on a shelf in the next room, and with George before me, asking me to read one of his favorites. I sent him up to bed, promising again that I would read *Watership Down*. "Along with three hundred and sixty-four other books," I added.

Two nights later I found myself downstairs at midnight, the only one in the house still awake, with that day's book just finished and now closed in my lap. I had read Paul Auster's *Man in the Dark*, and I scribbled into its margins, for posting later, "This book is perfect, a genuine communication from the heart." I sighed and leaned back against my old purple chair. I was getting used to this late-night reading. So much for the six hours between school buses, and my plan for getting my book read and my review written before the kids got home from school. The plan had changed, and now my days ended with a book in my lap. The experience of just me and my book under the light of one lamp was like sitting before a spotlighted stage in a dark theater. The whole performance went on just for me. No intermission, no interruptions, and every word illuminated.

Man in the Dark is a novel that imagines another world

mirroring our own. Two worlds coexisting: Auster uses the device to dig deeply into what keeps us going, what keeps us participating in the motions and the emotions of life. A man, his daughter, and his granddaughter are all facing their own private heartbreaks. They are unsure of how to go on and wavering as to the necessity of even trying to go on. Why bother? And then, in the prose of a lesser-known poet, they find a single sentence that makes perfect sense: "The weird world rolls on."

The world shifts, and lives change. Without warning or reason, someone who was healthy becomes sick and dies. An onslaught of sorrow, regret, anger, and fear buries those of us left behind. Hopelessness and helplessness follow. But then the world shifts again—rolling on as it does—and with it, lives change again. A new day comes, offering all kinds of possibilities. Even with the experience of pain and sorrow set deep within me and never to be forgotten, I recognize the potent offerings of my unknown future. I live in a "weird world," shifting and unpredictable, but also bountiful and surprising. There is joy in acknowledging that both the weirdness and the world roll on, but even more, there is resilience.

The night before Thanksgiving, I had a dream. I dreamed I was in Cambridge, England, walking through the Wren Library. I ran into Anne-Marie, alive and well.

"I don't know what to read now," I said to her. "Should I read a sixteenth-century philosopher or the new edition of Chaucer's *Canterbury Tales* that just came out? What do you think?" Just days before I'd read the deeply atmospheric and scary *Man in the Picture* by Susan Hill, set in Cambridge. It made sense I was dreaming about Cambridge. But where did the sixteenth-century philosopher come from? And why *The Canterbury Tales*?

In my dream, the choices I offered didn't puzzle my sister. They only made her smile.

Giving me that look of hers—the one where she pursed her lips and drew in her eyebrows, signaling acute brain activity—Anne-Marie said to me, "I'll have to think about that. I'll get back to you." She turned around and walked away. She was wearing her Yves Saint-Laurent trench coat from the '80s, belted tightly around her middle. She turned to wave, and then she was gone.

When I woke up on Thanksgiving morning, I understood the world was rolling for me, asleep and awake. In its rolling, there was giving and there was taking. I was sure Anne-Marie would get back to me, philosopher or poet. Until then, I had a promise to keep.

The next day I read *Watership Down*, all 476 pages of it.

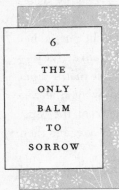

6

THE
ONLY
BALM
TO
SORROW

Now, lodged in the body of a living person, I could remember everything, everywhere, every time. It was as if I were on my way back, on a return journey.

MIA COUTO,
Under the Frangipani

WHEN I RETURNED TO THE HOSPITAL AFTER GETTING THE call that my sister had died, I found my father rocking back and forth on the couch in her hospital room, repeating over and over, "Three in one night." I had no idea what those words meant, and when I asked Natasha about it later, she didn't know either. I wanted to ask my father, but at the same time I couldn't take any more sadness. Jack's sister Mary died in June after a long illness, and I felt as if I were underwater, drowning in tears. I couldn't go to Mary's funeral, terrified that I would submerge for good into grief and darkness. In July we scattered Anne-Marie's ashes in the ocean off Fire Island. In late September, we held her memorial service.

The service was held at New York University's Institute of Fine Arts, in the grand rooms of its Millionaires' Row mansion on Fifth Avenue. Friends and family spoke; then Marvin ran a slide show of photos while a trio of cellist, pianist, and violinist played Beethoven. More friends spoke, and Marvin ended the service with his own memories from the life he shared with Anne-Marie.

Memories of Anne-Marie would be all we could have of her.

We no longer had a future with her to look forward to. Sharing our recollections of time spent with Anne-Marie was part of keeping hold of her, although I didn't realize it at the time. I was there to celebrate her life that afternoon. I didn't understand the importance of ensuring her remembrance. I only realized three years later, when reading *The Book of Chameleons* by José Eduardo Agualusa, the significance of the sharing of memories. And the danger of not sharing memories at all.

In *The Book of Chameleons*, main character Felix Ventura's profession is to replace the memories of his clients with new memories. Most of his clients use their new memories to support an exalted identity. They are trying to get away from their pasts of poverty and inconsequence in order to move up in the world. Ventura has godlike gifts of re-creation. He molds around each client a new skin, unsheddable and opaque. But not all histories can be traded in and discarded. The past will rise up to be acknowledged: "The smell is still there, the sound of the child crying."

A book of fiction, *The Book of Chameleons* is based on the very real atrocities committed in Angola's struggle for independence from Portugal. Agualusa imagines what would happen if victims and perpetrators sought to forget the horrors and uses his story to underscore the impossibility of such forgetting. By the end of the book, remembrance is the only pathway, painful as it is, to a settlement with the past: "I'm at peace at last. I fear nothing. I yearn for nothing."

The day after reading Agualusa's book, I picked up another book translated from the Portuguese, Mia Couto's *Under the Frangipani*. Couto is a writer from Mozambique, a country, like Angola, brutally governed during its years as a Portuguese colony. *Under the Frangipani* tells the story of a murder investigation told from the point of view of a man who is dead but who has taken up residence in the body of the investigator. The dead man cares less about his own death than he does about "killing the world of the past." He fears that the leaders of Mozambique, having fought for independence, no longer believe in the old African ways, the culture and traditions of their ancestors. Instead, they are rushing to catch up with the West, and allowing the past to be forgotten. They are becoming "people without a history, people who live by imitation." In contrast, the dead man is regaining memories through the body of the inspector, and he is grateful: "Now, lodged in the body of a living person, I could remember everything, everywhere, every time. It was as if I were on my way back, on a return journey." He remembers the good and the bad, and finds validity for his own life in both. By taking that "return journey"—looking backward—he finds peace.

When we were growing up, our parents told us bits and pieces about living through World War II in Europe. Our mother grew up in Antwerp and remembers the Germans invading Belgium in May of 1940. Her father was mobilized to fight the Germans, and the whole family moved with him to France, staying with French families, some welcoming and some not so welcoming. My mother remembers walking along a beach in Brittany with her sister when a troop of Germans on motorcycles came roaring through, separating the sisters and terrifying my mother. She remembers driving through bombed-out towns in northern France and stopping at a house in Abbeville that had lost its entire front facade to bombing. The rooms gaped open like a dollhouse, its occupants long gone, having fled to the countryside. My mother needed to use the bathroom, so her mother sent her in. My mother entered a pristine bathroom, lined along one wall with a neat row of freshly polished shoes left behind by the fleeing family. She stepped past the shoes primly and did her business, surrounded by walls on three sides but only the open air in front of her.

Belgium surrendered to Germany within weeks, and the family returned to occupied Antwerp. Food shortages began, along with heavy rationing. There were no eggs in the city, no butter, and little sugar. My grandmother made marzipan out of mashed potatoes and almond extract; oatmeal contained more husks than oats; bread was brown and stringy with fiber; and milk was so diluted with water it was blue. The baby of the family, my uncle Peter, got most of the milk, but my mother didn't mind. Never a picky eater, she doesn't remember being hungry in the war. She was satisfied to eat up whatever was on her plate and told us she was the only one in her family who actually gained weight during the war.

In 1942, the Allied troops began bombings of Belgium, and blackouts were instituted. The entire city went dark at night, with all windows covered and no streetlamps lit. During the day my mother still walked the twenty minutes back and forth to her school, but now she always wore a package suspended from a string around her neck. The package comprised a handkerchief tied around a whistle and two cubes of sugar. The idea was that in the event of a bombing that left my mother under a pile of rubble, alive but trapped, she would put the handkerchief over her mouth to avoid breathing in dust, suck on the sugar cubes to sustain her energy, and blow like hell on the whistle to get rescued. Eventually my mother was packed off with her sister and brother to live in the countryside with her grandmother. She remembers sitting in a country classroom counting the lice on the head of the boy in front of her.

We understood that life in Belgium, while hard under German occupation, was still easier than it had been for my father, living under a succession of occupying forces, all of them oppressive. In 1939 Germany invaded Poland. Under a secret pact signed with Russia, Poland was divided up and Russia took over Belarus. Two years later, when Hitler broke his pact with Stalin, Germany marched east and took control of Belarus. When the tide turned against Germany in 1944, the Russians came swarming in again.

My father was a country boy, a farmer's child in a family of ten siblings. His father had fields of rye and wheat, and also orchard after orchard of cherries, pears, and apples. During the first winter of the first Soviet occupation, the coldest winter on record, the fruit trees all froze up and died. The years of Soviet occupation were hard, with the threats of deportation, collectivization, and starvation always hovering. My father continued to go to school and was now taught by Soviets. His schoolbooks were taken away one morning when the teachers realized the books contained photos of politicians, generals, and marshals who had since been executed by Stalin and removed from official Soviet history. The students spent fewer days in the classroom and more days engaged in hard labor, moving stones for roads and hauling lumber.

I remember that when I was still very young, my father often told me about when he saw his first airplane. It was a beautiful Sunday in June 1941, and my father lay out in a meadow, gazing up into the sky and daydreaming. All of a sudden he heard a roar. He sat up in disbelief as a silver plane screeched across the blue beyond. I was much older when my father explained to me that it was a German plane, and that the Germans were invading Belarus. The Red Army scrambled, trying to get out before the Germans arrived. An old Red Army officer, quoting a Russian proverb, warned my father: "The wolf will have to pay for the sheep's tears." My father feared that once again the

Belarusians would be the sheep. One week later the *Wehrmacht* arrived in the village.

A group of German officers on bicycles stopped at my grandfather's farm. One of the bikes needed repairing, and they'd heard that my grandfather had the tools necessary to fix it. My father was one of the few in his small village who spoke German, and so his father sent him out to help the officers. He stood out in the yard handing out tools and taking parts and bolts from the Germans as they dismantled the bike. Whatever had been wrong was fixed, and the Germans began to put the bike back together. But the bolts fastening one of the pedals in place were missing. The officers began scurrying through the yard, looking everywhere for the bolts. My father followed behind them, trying to help. But the bolts just could not be found. The officers finally shrugged off the loss, and mounted their bikes. As they rode away, one of the soldiers rode off-kilter, trying to keep up on his one-pedaled bike. Later that night my father found the bolts in his pocket, where he had put them and forgotten about them. He didn't know whether to cry at his close call with German discipline or to laugh with relief.

As we girls grew older and learned more about the war in school and in the books we read, we began to ask questions. *Did you know anyone who was taken by the Germans to a concentration camp? Were you ever actually in a bombing? Did you ever see a dead person?* My mother didn't know any families who were deported. One good friend who was Jewish went into hiding and survived the war. My mother was never caught in a bombing, but a school just outside Antwerp was bombed by the Allies in 1943. The target was a car factory being used by the Luftwaffe to repair planes, but the Allies missed the factory and hit St. Lutgardis School instead. More than two hundred children were killed; only eighteen survived. I wonder if those children had worn little handkerchief packages around their necks.

When I was in law school, the movie *Look and See* was released in the United States. Set in Belarus during the last years of World War II, it is the most painful movie about war I have ever seen. Against a background of green fields and towering birch trees, the characters—played by Belarusian actors who look like they could be my family—suffer through hunger, fear, and torture and fight helplessly against being corralled for death marches, burnings, and killings. I cried every night for weeks afterward, thinking about that movie. When I finally flat out asked my father about what he had experienced in the war, he told me halting half stories. He just couldn't talk about it.

It was not until after the fall of the Berlin Wall in 1989 that my father began to share his stories of the war. Even then, he could not talk about his memories but instead committed them to words on paper. Working on an old typewriter that had been mine in high school, he began to type out the details of the horrors he had witnessed and heard about. He wrote about how his Jewish friends were kicked out of school once the Germans came and were made to wear yellow stars and work in the streets. Later they were taken to work camps. My father saw bodies lying on the street in a village. He saw a young man strung up to die. One day he walked past a field with a barn set at the end of the meadow. The barn was in flames and surrounded by German soldiers. Only when my father began to smell the roasting bodies did he understand that the barn was full of people, and that the doors had been barred closed against them. The smell made my father's knees buckle, and he stumbled to the ground, trying to get away. He had been studying ancient Rome in school, and the parallels between the atrocities committed by the ancient Romans against their enemies and what he saw in his own modern country horrified him.

My father wrote about how an uncle and aunt suspected of helping out Jewish friends were arrested by the occupying Germans and executed. Another uncle, suspected of being a Communist because he had taught in a Russian school, was taken away and never seen again.

We always knew that four of my father's ten siblings had died in World War II, but the details had been fuzzy. Only when my father began writing out his memories did we begin to learn more. My father's brother Peter was the first to die; he died in 1939 fighting the Germans after being drafted into the Polish army. And then, after my sister died, my father wrote about the horrible night in early December 1943 when three of his siblings died. *Three in one night.*

My father was away at school that night, in a town twenty-six kilometers from home. His brother George was there with him, having escaped from a German transport train that was taking him west to work in a German factory. The two brothers knew that Soviet partisans were roaming the countryside, staging sabotage maneuvers and planning attacks on the German armies, but they weren't worried. During the years of the Soviet occupation my grandfather, who owned a general store, managed to avoid deportation of the entire family to Siberia by keeping the local Russian officials well supplied with a private stock of good Polish vodka. Under the new occupation by the Germans, the family gave the Germans what they needed during the day, and the partisans came at night to take what they needed.

On that night in December, a group of partisans came to

the farm, but my grandfather was away. My grandmother was there at home, sick with fever and chills. Boris, thirty-two years old, Antonina, twenty-three years old, and fifteen-year-old Sergei were also at home that night. While my grandmother rested in a room off the kitchen, Boris, Antonina, and Sergei stayed up talking.

My father doesn't know who answered the door to the partisans. I imagine my grandmother waking in her sickbed to hear footsteps, a loud stomping of many boots over floorboards. Even the straw laid out on the floor to catch the dirt couldn't muffle the sound of those steps. There were maybe four or five partisans in the house, all men. My grandmother heard harsh Russian voices shouting at her children. She couldn't hear the words of Boris, Sergei, and Antonina, only the murmurings of their replies. Then she heard sounds she could not understand, not at first, not until she heard the pleading of Antonina. She heard muffled words, a supplication, then crying. She heard more sounds she could not understand. And then my grandmother heard sounds she understood too well. She heard gunshots, and the sound of weights falling heavily, one after the other, onto the floor. She heard shallow gasping, and silence. Silence and then a sudden, violent breaking of plates, chairs, glasses. Angry voices. The retreating stomps of boots going away.

My grandmother was left alone. When she came out into the kitchen, there was no sign of her children, only bloodstains on the floor amid the pieces of broken glass and ceramic and wood. She never saw her three children again. That night she walked sixteen kilometers to the police station in the next village, but no one could help her. The bodies had been taken away by the partisans and were never recovered.

When my sister died, my father's repeated lamentation, "Three in one night, three in one night," was his plea across the years to his mother. A plea of sympathy offered, a plea for help. My father just could not understand how my grandmother got through the next day, or the next, or the rest of her life after losing within minutes three entire lives of possibilities. My father couldn't understand how he would get through another day after losing his oldest daughter, one life still so full of things to do and to know. How could her life be over? How could his go on?

I tried to find my own understanding of how my grandmother managed to get through the day after her children were murdered, and the day after and the day after. How is it that she did not go mad? Knowing my father's story, knowing how his sister and brothers died, and how his mother, hiding in a room, had to listen to them die, unable to save them, I tried to understand the survival of those left alive. How is it that anyone can keep walking upright? How am I able to continue living, now that my sister is dead? The whole world should tremble and shake at every death, but if it did, we would never be still. The world would literally rock with death and sorrow. How is it that we hold on to the shell of the earth and of our lives, and go on?

After Anne-Marie died, sorrow became part of my life. I came slowly to realize that it was not going to go away. Sorrow is a violent smashing of reason, in that reason has no power over it. Everyone offering their palliatives—"She wouldn't want you to be sad" or "She lived a good life"—gave me sound reasons to stop my grieving, and yet I could not. Because how can anyone not rant and rave when the horror of death slams down?

But now, in reading my books of escape, I had found another way to respond. It was not a way to rid myself of sorrow but a way to absorb it. Through memory. While memory cannot take sorrow away or bring back the dead, remembering ensures that we always have the past with us, the bad moments but also the very, very good moments of laughter shared and meals eaten together and books discussed.

Remembering people who have died also gives dignity to the dead and respect to the lives they led. In *The Emigrants*, W. G. Sebald traces the lives of four men forced to emigrate from Germany because of economics or war. Sebald uses artifacts such as photographs, journals, letters, and notes of his visits with families and friends to present richly detailed and personal histories of alienation and struggle. Each man and each story is very different, but they share the same loss of identity: three of the men lost their German identity through the crimes of World War II, and one man lost his identity through sublimating his will to that of his employer. All the emigrants struggled to forge a new identity in their new land, but the displacement of self was just too much. As vividly as we see these men, thanks to Sebald's storytelling, they could not see themselves at all; they saw only ghosts, or shells, with nothing—or not enough—inside. Two finally chose suicide, another chose to annihilate himself through electroshock therapy, and a fourth is saved only by the painting he does in his studio in an abandoned warehouse, the dust of which eventually kills him with its toxicity.

The Emigrants is not a happy book, but it is a book absolutely resounding with life. If I put my finger on any page of the book, I felt the pulsing heartbeat of the lives Sebald recorded. It is the heartbeat he gave back to them, making them real for me. "Remembrance" for me means remembering someone with love or with respect. Remembrance is acknowledging that a life was lived. Sebald's book is a remembrance of four lives.

I was in my forties, reading in my purple chair. My father was in his eighties, and my sister was in the ocean, her ashes scattered there by all of us in swimsuits under a blue sky. And only now am I grasping the importance of looking backward. Of remembrance. My father finally wrote out his memories for a reason. I took on a year of reading books for a reason. Because words are witness to life: they record what has happened, and they make it all real. Words create the stories that become history and become unforgettable. Even fiction portrays truth: good fiction *is* truth. Stories about lives remembered bring us backward while allowing us to move forward.

The only balm to sorrow is memory; the only salve for the pain of losing someone to death is acknowledging the life that existed before. Remembering someone won't literally bring them back, and for one who died too young, memories are not enough to make up for all the possibilities of life that they lost out on. But remembrance is the bones around which a body of resilience is built. I think my father found an answer to how his mother continued on, and he found a way to go on himself. He wrote a history for me to read. Stories helped him, and stories were helping me, both the stories of my father and the stories in all the books I was reading.

The truth of living is proved not by the inevitability of death but by the wonder that we lived at all. Remembering lives from the past ratifies that truth, more and more so the older we get. When I was growing up, my father told me once, "Do not look for happiness; life itself is happiness." It took me years to understand what he meant. The value of a life lived; the sheer value of living. As I struggled with the sadness of my sister's death, I came to see that I was facing the wrong way and look-ing at the end of my sister's life and not at the duration of it. I was not giving remembrance its due. It was time to turn myself around, to look backward. By looking backward, I would be able to move forward. Time to begin a return journey to my own life, carried in part by the remembered life of my sister.

7

———

LOOKING

FOR

THE

STAR

*"May I tell you why it seems to me a good thing
for us, to remember wrong that has been done us?"*
"Yes."
"That we may forgive it."

CHARLES DICKENS,
The Haunted Man and the Ghost's Bargain

THE HOLIDAYS ARE AN EXCELLENT TIME FOR LOOKING backward. One of my earliest memories is of sitting on our golden couch (very modish in the 1960s) with my sisters beside me, while our father read to us from *The Christmas Story*. *The Christmas Story* was a book put out by the Metropolitan Museum of Art in 1966, the text coming from the Gospels of Matthew and Luke, and the illustrations provided by paintings from the Met's own collections.

My father read in a singsong voice that laid heavy then soft emphasis on the words. Looking back, I would describe his delivery as reminiscent of southern preachers I'd seen on television, but with a strong Belarusian accent.

The story my father read to us was strange and intoxicating. I was moved by its images and ideas: swaddling clothes; shepherds abiding in the field; good tidings of great joy, peace, good will toward men; and "Lo, the star, which they saw in the East." Long before I had children of my own and experienced the rush of absolute love and faith brought by a newborn, I understood how a helpless baby lying in straw could inspire selfless and unbounded love. I could picture the poor shepherds out there alone in the dark on a cold night. Suddenly they hear music, and they look up at the starlit sky. Angels fly above them, and a huge star beckons. They are filled with certainty: life can be good, and joyful, and peaceful. Love and hope are shared and by being shared, are spread. Peace on Earth brought by a child and signaled by a star.

It all made perfect sense to me as a child of the 1960s. I would listen to the story and then go outside and look for a huge star in the night sky. I was looking for a sign that war would be over, the Vietnam War and the Cold War and all the other wars that as a child I suspected were being fought all over, far from my own backyard but in the yards of children somewhere. Looking for the star in the sky became my own private Christmas ritual, my own search for peace.

My mother found peace in the crèche scene she created every year. Along with my father's reading and the play we girls put on every Christmas Eve, her five-story crèche was one of my favorite holiday traditions. She created her elaborate world of small figures in the built-in bookshelves that lined our fireplace in Evanston. Books would be turned on their sides to make valleys and stacked up high to make hills. My mother would lay white cloths over the books, creating rolling landscapes in snow. Boughs cut from the Christmas tree were placed in the background. The space was now ready to be populated, and my mother would bring out her *santons*.

Small clay statuettes painted in bright colors, *santons* (originally made in Provence) represented all characters from traditional village life. Everyone was there, from the local priest wiping his forehead with a handkerchief to a woman with a basket of fruit on her head, from a young mother on her way to go shopping with a hamper on her arm to a farmer boy with a pig under one arm. There were churches set up high in the hills made from books, and farms placed in the hollows, with hay-stacks and farm animals. There was even a monastery, built by me during seventh-grade woodshop and peopled by reformed women of the night, still dressed in flamboyant clothes but with reverence on their painted faces.

My mother created a stream running down one hillside out of silver Christmas tree icicles, and placed a fisherman on its banks. She made a pond out of a small mirror, with geese gathered at its edge. One year Anne-Marie brought home a painted metal figure of Sonja Henie to skate across the mirror pond.

Circles of animals surrounded the nativity scene. A fox, a bear, a family of mice, a lion, all sorts of cats, a porcupine: these animals and others approached Joseph, Mary, and little baby Jesus, lying in his manger, across puffs of white linen. My grandmother gave my parents the nativity starter kit when they married. The animals and the surrounding one hundred-plus *santon* figurines milling happily around, above and below the happy family, had been bought over the years.

Not only was earthly life represented in my mother's crèche scene but heaven and hell as well. Heaven was set up on the highest shelf, in an arch just below the ceiling. God reigned there, visible as a squat wooden figure painted in gold and blue, placed among all the singing angels. A full angel band played in the background. Cat angels, fat angels, and short and tall angels filled in the sides of the shelf. My mother put a figure representing Homer in one corner of heaven, and in the other corner, a glass man at a glass piano represented Mozart.

Hell took up the lowest bookshelf and spread along the floorboards. My mother started building hell only when we got a little older, but once started, hell took off. It soon became overpopulated with little red figures, including a red-sequined

Mickey Mouse and tiny red devils made by Anne-Marie out of clay, their arms lifted in friendly waves and with the sweetest of smiles pricked into their chubby faces. Friends brought Day of the Dead figures from Mexico. A toy snake made its way into hell and never came out again.

I have never missed a Christmas with my parents, but Anne-Marie stayed away a few times, including the Christmas before she died. She and Marvin, along with two friends, went to India that year for three weeks of travel. The worst tsunami in history rolled through the Indian Ocean on December 26, 2004. I knew Anne-Marie hadn't planned on going down to the beaches in southern India, but when for two days we hadn't heard from her, I began to fear the worst. What if they had changed their plans? What if they had gone to the beach and gotten caught up in one of the huge waves? When Anne-Marie finally called my parents, I felt relief, and stupidity for having worried. Twenty-one days later, back in New York, Anne-Marie felt a lump on her abdomen. We were hit with a tidal wave, but not the one I had worried about.

The Christmas after Anne-Marie died, my mother didn't want to put up her crèche scene. Natasha and I begged her to do it.

"Do it for the boys," we said. "Do it for us." Finally, she agreed to display her figures in their winter wonderland. The layout had changed since my parents' move to New York City, but it was as magnificent as ever. The *santons* spread in villages across the fireplace mantel, with the nativity scene to the left. New additions included a fox bringing an offering to the baby in his teeth, and a four-sided fountain for one of the village squares. Heaven reveled on a high chest to the side, and hell hunkered down in the open cavity of the nonworking fireplace. I brought my mother a figure of an angel with flowing hair resting on her stomach and reading a book. My mother placed her in heaven, beside Homer.

Jack and I had our own holiday Christmas traditions, going back to the first days of our relationship. We first kissed on New Year's Eve, and the following year, we bought our first Christmas tree together. The tree was small and skinny enough to carry home the thirty-plus blocks from Little Italy to West Twenty-first Street. We put twisty green wire with red berries on the ends onto the branches—our first ornaments—and when Jack's daughter, Meredith, and I baked Christmas cookies that turned out like lead, we painted them, drilled holes through the top, and hung them up too. Over the years the size of our trees went from smaller to bigger to smaller again, depending on the size of our living space.

The year Meredith moved into our two-bedroom apartment on West Eighty-first Street and began living with us full-time, we bought a very small tree. Jack and I had brought our bed into the living room to give his fourteen-year-old daughter her own bedroom, leaving three boys to share the other bedroom. There was no space for anything but a tabletop tree that year. Two years later, when we left that apartment for a town house with leaking walls, a partial roof, and no working kitchen, we bought a huge tree to reach the top of the parlor-floor ceiling.

Since we moved to the suburbs, our tree has been getting bigger and bigger. We went every year to a farm on the other side of town, with its acres and acres of white spruce, blue spruce, and Douglas fir. The fields of trees roll right alongside I-95, and this year we once again picked our tree against the roar of trucks. Maybe it was the trucks, maybe it was the cacophony of six different voices with six different opinions as to the right tree for us, maybe it was our crazy thirst for that great pine smell, but we'd long lost our ability to gauge what a tree in a field would look like when we brought it home to stand alone in our front hall.

"Are you sure?" the tree-farm volunteer asked us when we pointed out our chosen tree.

"Yes, definitely," I said. Jack drove the car around while the volunteer hacked through the tree's ten-inch trunk. When it was finally on top of our car, sap dripping down the back, I saw what the young guy had been talking about. The branches of the tree drooped down over both sides, blocking the windows and the back doors.

I got in the car and checked the view. "I can see clear out the front. Let's go, boys!" The boys climbed in over the front seat, and off we went. Getting the tree off the car when we got home wasn't easy. We pushed and pulled it down to the ground, and then dragged the tree over to the front door.

"Lift it," Jack bellowed. "Don't drag it. Lift! Lift!"

Four of us shoved the tree up the front steps while Jack and Michael pulled from ahead. Accompanied not by carols but by swear words we'd vowed never to use around the boys but used every single Christmas at tree-getting time, we got the tree into the hallway. I placed the crowning decoration of a blond angel on the top branch (where did we get that hideous thing?), and we positioned ourselves to haul the tree upright. More pushing and pulling and more swearing, and we got it into the two-ton iron stand. The tree tottered, scraping the surrounding walls and ceiling and leaving long marks in green and brown.

"Is it scratching anywhere?" Jack asked from his position down by the stand.

"No, no," I answered. "Everything's good up here." The tree steadied and stood. Jack tightened the bolts along the trunk and moved away.

We had outdone ourselves, again. This year's tree was so tall that its top poked into the chandelier hanging from the second-floor ceiling. A light from the chandelier went right up the angel's skirts, illuminating her from a whole new angle. Branches of the tree spread out across the staircase and filled the front hallway, making passage up or across difficult. It was as if the tree had come first and we had arrived second, assembling ourselves, our house, and our lives around this overtall, overpowering tree. I had images of a squirrel poking its head out, just like in the movie *Christmas Vacation*. Where am I? the furry little creature wonders, just before he leaps onto my head.

I tracked strands of colored lights through the tree's branches, then let my kids loose with the ornaments. By nightfall our tree—our lodestar, our reason for the season—was back in full-reign mode. It was no longer too big. It was now just right. The cats took their places under the low branches, while we all moved to sit in the living room. We could get only a partial view; the tree was so big there was no place in the house to see it fully. All views were partial, shot through with sparkling color, blazing lights, and a background of deep green.

Over the next few days I brought out the old record albums, *Go Tell It on the Mountain*, *A Bing Crosby Christmas*, and excerpts from Handel's *Messiah*. I hauled down from the attic our crate of Christmas books and pawed through them, each book sparking a memory of past Christmases. We had plenty of children's books, and my favorites were well-worn, marked with sticky fingerprints and torn corners: *Peter Spier's Christmas*, drawings of one family's yearly rituals; *Christmas Without a Tree* by Elizabeth B. Rodger, about a generous little pig; and *The Christmas Crocodile* by Bonny Becker, illustrated by David Small, and used by me as a blueprint for what I wanted my house to look like during the holidays (*before* the crocodile ate everything). We also had classics like Dickens's *A Christmas Carol* and Lois Lenski's *Christmas Stories*—I still have the original copy that I'd received when I was ten. And I had our family's copy of the Metropolitan Museum of Art's *Christmas Story*, with its lovely words and beautiful paintings.

Most years I reread all of the books dragged down from the attic, from the simplest children's book to the *Ghost Stories of Christmas* collection. Not this year. I wouldn't have time this year, not with my book-a-day schedule. I was worried that I wouldn't have time for many of our Christmas rituals, what with my reading. But I made plans to do the things we really liked to do, and I figured the rest would get worked out as we went along.

I chose to read some new Christmas books—the terribly boring *Abbot's Ghost* by Louisa May Alcott; Jimmy Carter's endearingly boring *Christmas in Plains*; and *The Haunted Man and the Ghost's Bargain* by Charles Dickens. The man in Dickens's story is haunted by memories of past wrongs done to him, and by past sufferings: "I see them in the fire, but now. They come back to me in music, in the wind, in the dead stillness of the night, in the revolving years."

A ghost who appears to be the doppelgänger of the haunted man offers him a deal. The double offers to take away all bad memories, leaving a blank space. He promises a void where once there were shadows of the past. "Memory is my curse; and, if I could forget my sorrow and my wrong, I would!" And so the haunted man makes the bargain. Out go all memories, and with them, all the man's capacity for tenderness, empathy, understanding, and caring. Our haunted man realizes too late that by giving up memories, he has become a hollow and miserable man, and a spreader of misery to all whom he touches.

Because it is Christmas and because he is Dickens's creation, the haunted man gets a chance to renege on the bargain with the ghost, get back his memories, and spread holiday cheer.

I loved the story, convinced as I had become of the importance of memories. But I came up hard against the conclusion posited by Dickens: the reason it is good to remember a past wrong is so that "we may forgive it." How could I ever forgive the taking of Anne-Marie's life?

The weekend before Christmas my parents and Natasha came to Westport to make the gingerbread men we make every year, a tradition dating back to when I was in elementary school. Our gingerbread men reflect our interests. When I was little, I made snowmen iced with white frosting to a one-inch thickness. I've always had a sweet tooth, and I took any license to indulge. When I was a teenager, I made a David Bowie gingerbread man, using red-hot cinnamon dots for the lightning bolt across his face; Anne-Marie made a Lady Godiva; and Natasha made volleyball players wearing our high school colors. Around the same time my mother began her tradition of making an anatomically correct Adam and Eve, and a gorgeously endowed mermaid. This year my kids tended toward the gory, using red sprinkles for blood and decapitating their gingerbread men so frequently it was as if we were making an army of martyred saints.

Days passed on with reading and writing, Christmas card making and sending, carol singing, school parties, and one car accident. I was hit from behind when I stopped for a school bus. Luckily, I came out just a little stiff in the neck, and the car was drivable. Repairs would have to wait until after the holidays.

On Christmas Eve, friends came for dinner. The evening ended with dancing on the kitchen table. Peter was in charge of the music, the husbands were responsible for photos, and rest of us—two mothers and six kids—were four feet off the ground and whooping it up. Christmas morning came early, the boys eager to see what Santa brought them. While Jack drove into New York City to pick up my family for our usual celebration of eating, drinking, and eating and drinking some more, I wrote up my review of *The Love of the Last Tycoon* by F. Scott Fitzgerald, read the day before. The review was posted by the time Jack got back with my parents, Natasha, and her boyfriend, Phillip. Christmas eating and drinking and talking and toasting and celebrating began.

It was after ten o'clock on Christmas night when I sat down with my book for the day. The kids were asleep upstairs, my father and Jack were watching a movie in the family room, and my mother and I sat in the living room, seated in a strategic position, both by the fire and with a great view of the tree. Its lights glowed in the darkness of the front hallway. I stoked up the logs in the fireplace and brought my mother a glass of port and myself a mug of hot chocolate doctored liberally with Tia Maria.

I tuned in to the crazy story of *The Love Song of Monkey* by Michael Graziano. A man immobilized in a coma and sunk twenty thousand leagues beneath the sea finally has the time to think about his life. As he says, "There is no place on earth better suited for meditation than the mid-ocean ridge."

"Mama," I said, reaching across to touch my mother on the arm. "This book, it's about a guy who stays underwater—he can't die, but he can't get out of the water for years either. He just thinks all about his life. And now, that's how it is for me."

"Yes?" She was always willing to give me the benefit of the doubt.

"It's like my year of reading is a similar state of suspension, and I am also plunged twenty thousand leagues under—but under a pile of books. And for me, there is no better place for meditation than with all my books. I too finally have time to think about my life."

"And what are you thinking about?"

"That this has been a great Christmas. Because I did only what I really wanted to do—our family did the great stuff, like having you here and making the gingerbread men. I skipped making three varieties of cookies, and I read a book instead. And then I had time to read another one! And I didn't obsess over our Christmas card. I didn't go crazy with outdoor lights. I just hung some strands over the front porch, leaving the bushes unlit. I let the kids decorate our tree on their own, and I gave them free rein with the rest of the house."

I pointed over to the play tables covered with white cotton and displaying mixed-up villages of nativity scenes of all shapes, sizes, and nationalities (my own collection), plastic Santas and elves, reindeer, and camels, along with wooden rabbits, birds, one dog, an assortment of miniature toy soldier nutcrackers, and an ark my father had carved for the boys, which was now covered in colored sparkles and surrounded by holly branches. It was not quite my mother's crèche scene, but it was beautiful in its own way.

"And I have thought a lot about Anne-Marie."

My mother's face contracted. Then she shook her head. "I think about her all the time," she said. "How much she would have liked to see the boys as they grow up."

"I know." My eyes were filling with tears, but I went on talking. "And they do remember her, too. I think they always will."

"I hope so."

"This reading, it makes me see how we do remember, all the

time, the people we've loved. They become part of us—they are part of us. Anne-Marie is part of all this."

My mother listened.

"For this one year, Mama, I am staying twenty thousand leagues below the surface of what would have been my normal, overscheduled, overcontrolled life. I have Anne-Marie to thank for this. I am underwater, swimming with the authors of all the books I've been reading and sucking up the oxygen of all their words, and she is there too. The lives in the books are breathing life into me, new life. And helping me learn how to keep her alive. In me."

My mother nodded, her face tight, her eyes looking down. I knew that the way she missed Anne-Marie and longed for her to be with us was too painful for her to talk about. I felt the pain instead, in the sharpening of the air around us, in the heightening of the burn from the fireplace. There was a sudden intensity of living marked by remembering a death. And I knew, for my mother, she wished she could exchange her life for that death, and bring my sister back. But there was no such bargain to be made.

I felt a constriction deep within my throat. Neither my mother nor I would take the bargain offered by the ghost in Dickens's story—we held on to our memories of Anne-Marie with all our might—but in our remembering of Anne-Marie, was there a place for forgiveness? Rolling forward, looking backward. Did I also have to forgive the death of my sister?

Forgiveness is an elevated form of acceptance, an acknowledgment that life is not fair: "I forgive you, life, for the shitty deal you handed my sister." I couldn't do that. I accepted that I was alive and that Anne-Marie was dead. I accepted that no square deal would be offered, nor could one be made. But forgiveness? Something was holding me back.

I turned off all the lights in the living room and moved to sit next to my mother on the couch. We sat together for a long time in the dark, looking at my oversize lit-up tree. Years ago I'd gone out in the dark looking for the huge star in the sky. Maybe the star I'd been looking for in the sky all those years ago was actually here. In the tree. In my family. In all these books. In all the memories I carried inside me.

Peace on Earth.

Good tidings of great joy.

It wasn't forgiveness. But it was a beginning.

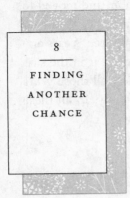

8

———

FINDING
ANOTHER
CHANCE

Once it perches on one's shoulder, guilt is not easily shrugged off.

MARTIN CORRICK,
By Chance

AT THE MOMENT WHEN I STOOD BESIDE MY SISTER'S DEATH-bed and heard my father crying, saw the hand of my mother clenching the white sheet covering Anne-Marie's body, I thought only of how to take my next breath, how to go on into the next moment of being alive, when Anne-Marie no longer was. But underneath my reacting brain, deep in the recesses of matter and memory and motivation, guilt was percolating. As the days went on, I felt the weight of it, so heavy and so unwieldy. I struggled with it, turning it this way and that, trying to understand. My rational self knew that I wasn't responsible for her death. My irrational self was not so sure. As months and then years passed, the guilt persisted. I reacted by living as fast and as hard as I could, figuring that by living double I was making it all up to Anne-Marie, living a life full of experiences that she would never have.

In the book *By Chance* by Martin Corrick, James Watson Bolsover is also a man burdened with guilt. Two deaths weigh upon his life, the death of his wife and the death of a child. Bolsover struggles with his remorse, fighting against it with reason and with anger, with sadness and with resignation, for "once it perches on one's shoulder, guilt is not easily shrugged off." His wife's death, owing to illness, clearly was not his fault, and the child's death was an accident. Yet he believes he might have eased the illness or prevented the accident. Without an easy resolution of either innocence or guilt, Bolsover suffers.

Bolsover tries to find an explanation for the two deaths, to uncover some reason they had to happen or if they could have been avoided. He searches for answers in books. At the beginning of *By Chance*, he asks the question, "If fiction is not concerned to understand, what is its subject? Is its purpose merely to pass the time?" but he already knows the answer. The purpose of great literature is to reveal what is hidden and to illuminate what is in darkness.

I was right there with Bolsover on his search for understanding, rooting alongside him for a why and wherefore for death, and hoping that he might find relief from his agonizing pain of responsibility and, in finding this relief, show me a way to ease my own. Bolsover felt guilt as a clawing into his shoulder. I felt it closer inside me, a sharpness scratching hard against my heart. My still beating heart. Beating only by chance. The chance that felled my sister but kept me alive.

Anne-Marie didn't like me much when I was a kid. She had good reasons. I was a bratty little sister. I went into her room when she wasn't home and took things for myself. I borrowed clothes—she always had better clothes than I did; she knew how to pick out good things—and wore them to school. After I wore a shirt of hers, I remember stuffing it into the back of her closet and claiming ignorance when she asked if I'd seen it.

One day I found Anne-Marie's diary and read it. I teased her when she got home about Scott Goodman, the neighbor she had a crush on. The truth was that everyone had a crush on Scott, including me, because he was tall and good-looking and very, very nice. The fact that Anne-Marie liked him was the surprising part. Her tastes usually ran counter to the popular stream of likes and dislikes. She was not a rebel but rather an iconoclast. She was sophisticated and discriminating in ways far beyond what might be expected of a sixteen-year-old midwestern girl. She took the teasing about Scott by hitting me back with sharp insults about the tiny size of my brain and the large size of my behind, and she hid her diary where I could never find it again. Anne-Marie didn't tell my parents about my snooping around and my teasing. She was no tattletale.

But I was. I told on her when I found cigarettes in the bathroom, pleading with my mother that I was worried about Anne-Marie's health. But I wasn't really, not then. I just wanted to get her in trouble. I wanted her to pay attention to me, her puny little sister. Any attention, even her caustic insults, was better than nothing. Later, when she got meaner and faster with her insults, I wanted payback for the hurt she caused me. Now I can see that it was I who started the fights between us. I was using the only power I had, the power to pester and to irritate. Anne-Marie was bigger, smarter, and so much better looking than me. But I won the annoying game, hands down.

As far as sibling dynamics went, Natasha was the sister I played with and Anne-Marie was the sister I bothered. Not that there wasn't solidarity among the three of us when required. One summer when we were driving through France, my father stopped our rental car at a gas station to fill up. Anne-Marie was by the open window, playing with her little red-haired troll named Troll. Just as my father pulled out of the station to drive back onto the highway, Anne-Marie dropped Troll out the window. My father would not go back to save Troll. We were on a highway with no turnoffs coming soon, and we couldn't delay our trip for a doll.

"But it's Troll!" Anne-Marie wailed. Natasha and I joined in, crying and crying for miles. We cried for Anne-Marie, bereft without her troll, and for Troll, all alone now in a strange country.

Troll was replaced by a large Steiff rabbit, and later Rabbit was replaced by a twelve-inch-long, amply stuffed lion named Lion. Lion had shiny brown eyes, a luxurious golden mane, and a soft yellow belly. Anne-Marie would hold him in one hand and use her fingers to move his arms up and down, giving him gestures as she made him talk. Lion was her alter ego. Lion could say anything—transmitted through a squeaky version of Anne-Marie's own voice—and because he was witty and quick, everyone would laugh at him. Even I laughed at him, despite the fact that his most effective lines were at my expense. I'd be talking about the Mrs. Piggle-Wiggle books by Betty MacDonald, one of my favorite series, and he'd cut in. "Wiggle, wiggle. I like that. Add a plop, plop and it can be my new nickname for you . . . 'cause that's what you look like when you walk. Plopplopwigglewiggle."

One afternoon when I was in seventh grade I got on a town bus to go home from school. I don't remember why I needed to take a bus that day. Maybe I'd stayed after school and didn't want to walk all the way home. It was only a thirty-minute walk, but maybe I was tired or thought it might get dark soon. What I do remember is thinking that the bus route was strange. For some reason the bus was heading into downtown Evanston. I figured it would turn around there and then head back north to my part of town.

The bus stopped for a moment by the huge parking garage downtown that also served as the main bus depot. I looked out the window to see Anne-Marie there on the sidewalk. She saw me at the same time, and her eyes widened. She started waving at me and yelling. When the bus started to roll away, she began running alongside it, screaming, "Stop! Stop!" The bus stopped, and Anne-Marie leaped on board. "Get off," she said to me. "You're on the wrong bus."

I had gotten on a bus heading to the Howard Street bus station in Chicago. The Howard Street station was in a seedy neighborhood of dimly lit bars, iron-barred liquor stores, dirty pawnshops, and broken-down apartment buildings. For a twelve-year old girl with no money, arriving at Howard Street as evening fell dark and cold around her, the bus station would have been the most terrifying place on earth.

"You saved my life," I babbled as I started crying and shaking. Anne-Marie drew her arms around me.

"Don't be stupid."

But I knew that she had saved me. I was a horrid brat, and yet she had run after the bus that could have taken me out of her life forever and got me off. She might not like me, but she did love me. Together, we took the right bus home. I sat next to my sister and vowed to myself that I would never go through her room again, I would never tattle on her or spy on her. I had thought Anne-Marie was better than me before, but now I was sure of it. She was not only smart and beautiful; she had a generous heart, willing to forgive me and to save me. Natasha was my buddy, my pal with whom I played, the sister I turned to after a bad dream, who would let me sleep beside her. But Anne-Marie became my gold standard of achievement, the one whose approval I sought even more than my parents'. Up she went on a pedestal, and for me, she never really came down again.

In Per Petterson's book *To Siberia*, a brother and a sister living in North Jutland during the years surrounding World War ll face extreme hardship and family heartbreak. Because they have each other, they survive. But then they become separated. The brother, deeply involved in the Resistance, has to run away from their Nazi-occupied town. Now the girl is alone. She is no longer entwined and in tune with her brother. She is no longer protected or sustained by him. Her life pales: "I am twenty-three and there is nothing left. Only the rest."

What did Petterson mean with those words, "only the rest"? For me, the words mean that for the rest of the girl's life she will be alone, living on in an existence without her brother. I understood that. I had shared my whole life with my sister, and then suddenly we were not sharing it any longer. I found it hard to imagine a life without her. How could my life still be a full life? No one could ever make up for the person who had gone.

Anne-Marie once quoted Ezra Pound to me, that what we love best "remains, and the rest is dross." What she didn't add was Pound's promise, "What thou lov'st well shall not be reft from thee." Not even death will take what I love best from me? The sister in *To Siberia* lives a long life, and writes about her brother. She transforms their lost history of unity into a recorded story of love. In writing words, she found her brother again. In reading words, in reading books, I was finding my sister again.

I was reminded of Anne-Marie in the characters I was meeting in all my days of books. She was the kind of heroine authors like to put in their books, with her quiet strength and resilience, her utter lack of petty or trivial concerns, and the superlative combination of her beauty and her intelligence. Anne-Marie had her negative traits, but even those always seemed to me to be übertraits. Her caustic wit was knife sharp and accurate, but never directed toward anyone who couldn't take it (she was never cruel), and her impatience with idiocy might have been overblown but it was never misplaced. Even when I was the idiot at the end of her thrusts of anger, I rarely felt wronged—I just wished for a little more sympathy. And always, eventually, the sympathy would come.

The main character in Thomas Pynchon's *Crying of Lot 49* is Oedipa Maas. She is nervy but also nervous, intelligent but self-questioning, honest and serious, an optimist but no pushover. Add in that she is good-looking, with long legs and long hair, and she *was* Anne-Marie. When I read that book, I pictured Oedipa as my sister, and my interest in her fate grew.

Anne-Marie was Aurora in Almudena Solana's *The Curriculum Vitae of Aurora Ortiz*, a woman who lives on her own terms, fully but quietly. She doesn't understand why people rush around without thinking or exploring: "Why are people so afraid of thinking? Why don't they ever leave time to reflect? There's nothing wrong with tranquility; nor emptiness, vertigo, or even unhappiness. I think that these things are the first steps to precede the birth of a new thought. This is why I like to read." Again, I pictured Anne-Marie saying these words, offering counsel to me. Slow down and think. Read a book. I was doing that.

Anne-Marie was the one I pictured for the rebellious gardener in *The Howling Miller* by Arto Paasilinna. No one can tell Sanelma whom to love and whom to forsake, and both her bravery and her loyalty reminded me of my sister. Anne-Marie was the New Year Sister in Nathaniel Hawthorne's short story "The Sister Years," a woman with "so much promise and such an indescribable hopefulness in her aspect that hardly anybody could meet her without anticipating some very desirable thing—some long sought after good—from her kind offices." Anne-Marie could look forbidding, but when she smiled, her features lightened up to those of a girl, a happy, bright girl expecting and offering all the wonders of the world.

Anne-Marie was sometimes deeply unsure of herself—strange or new situations always made her nervous—but when the truly terrible circumstances of cancer slammed into her, she responded with an iron will overlaid with grace and calm. Again like a heroine from a book, Anne-Marie thrust herself in front of the moving train that was cancer and tried to protect me from its reality. She absorbed all of its truth and all of its horror on her own, by herself. It makes me shudder now to think of how she must have felt, scared, angry, and helpless. I don't know if putting on the brave act for me helped her psychologically with her illness. Or if by taking on the burden of protecting me—as she always had—she doubled her own burden.

The guilt that was scratching away at me, the twist of a knife that woke me up in the middle of the night and made me wonder wherein my failure lay, came from how Anne-Marie bore the horror of her cancer. How alone she was. How I could not share the weight of her illness, or take it from her. And it was guilt for placing her on a pedestal all those years ago and not letting her down again. I was looking for resolution—innocence or guilt—just like Bolsover. And like Bolsover, I was looking for a reason or an explanation for why she had to die.

In *By Chance*, Bolsover comes to realize that "he is not a wicked man, but only a foolish one." The relief he finds is not in the absolution of his guilt but rather in the absolution of his life. He understands that he is lucky to be alive; it is only "by chance" that he is, while his wife and the child are dead. Bolsover resolves to take the chance offered and find what peace and joy he can, while he can. What else can he do but rise every morning to follow where "the sun has laid a blazing road of orange and gold"? He understands that "one must take control of one's life or become nothing but a broken branch, drifting in the current."

Guilt was the force holding me back from forgiving the death of Anne-Marie. Guilt was the barrier against accepting that I was alive, and she no longer was. My oldest, smartest, most beautiful sister had lost her own life, having long ago saved mine.

I had to forgive myself for living.

Toward the end of January, I read *Moonlight Shadow* by Banana Yoshimoto. Satsuki, a young woman whose boyfriend has been killed in a car accident, tries to assuage her pain by going out for long runs through her town. Every morning while out running, Satsuki stops for a rest on the bridge where she last saw her boyfriend. One morning she meets a woman on the bridge, and they begin a strange friendship: "Somewhere deep in my heart I felt I had known her long ago, and the reunion made me so nostalgic I wanted to weep tears of joy." Through this woman Satsuki is given a unique chance, the chance to see her boyfriend one last time, and to talk to him. She calls across the river, "Hitoshi, do you want to talk to me? I want to talk to you. I want to run over to your side, take you in my arms, and rejoice in being together again."

I read the book on a cold but sunny day. I was home all alone, the boys at school and Jack at work. The cats lay on the floor beside my chair in the squares of sun that came in through the windows. After finishing *Moonlight Shadow*, I sat back in my purple chair. If I had the chance to see Anne-Marie one last time, the chance Satsuki had with her beloved Hitoshi, would I ask her to forgive me for being the one who got to live? For not taking on the burden of cancer? No, of course not. Such questions would be self-serving and selfish, and would only cause pain to both of us. Instead, I would tell her the truth about what she had left behind in me. I would tell her how much I loved her. I would promise to bring her forth alive every day in my memories, and in my touching of the people, the objects, and the places she left behind. I would live, always with her in mind: I was not alone. "What thou lov'st well . . . ," I would remind her. And in that love which I carried forward, I would find forgiveness.

I went upstairs to my bedroom. Lion sat there on a bookshelf, on top of stacks of paperback mysteries. He was raggedy, his shiny eyes sagging in their sockets. His yellow mane had gone gray with dirt and time, and his belly was flat. A gold-and-orange ribbon wound around his neck, tied on by Anne-Marie after bringing him out of retirement when my kids were born. The ribbon helped keep his head up, given that most of his stuffing was gone. In Anne-Marie's hands, and with her voice, Lion entertained the boys. Once again, she'd had Lion make jokes at my expense, to my sons' delight and disbelief and uncontrollable giggles.

Now Lion lived on with me, voiceless but still present. I took Lion in my arms and gave him a kiss, right on top of his ratty little head. He was Anne-Marie's alter ego, and he will remain with me. As Anne-Marie remains with me, in my still-beating heart.

I've pushed blame away. My heart is scarred but clear of the scratching, clawing guilt that kept me from forgiving myself for living on when Anne-Marie could not. So where do I go now? What "blazing road of orange and gold" will I find to follow? *How* do I live?

I remembered the mandate from my very first book of the year, *The Elegance of the Hedgehog*, that I find moments of beauty, the "always within never." I was finding beauty, and recovering memories, and absolving guilt. Seeking peace and discovering joy. My path forward was clear to me. It was a path set ablaze by words, words made into sentences and paragraphs and chapters and books. My way was paved by books.

When you have possessed a book with mind and spirit, you are enriched. But when you pass it on you are enriched threefold.

HENRY MILLER,
The Books in My Life

ONE DAY IN MID-JANUARY AN INTERLOPER ARRIVED IN MY life. It was afternoon, and the kids were home from school. A good friend called and asked if she could stop by. She had a book for me to read. "I loved it," she said. My friend—or rather, the book offered out to me from her hands—was the interloper, an unexpected guest at my table of books.

Three months into my book-a-day project, and I was into a good rhythm of reading and writing. January was almost over, and the postholiday, midwinter blahs never had a chance with me this year. I was too caught up in reading great books and in the challenge of writing about them every day. Every morning I posted my review of the book I'd read the day before. Then I walked over to my bookcase and looked over books I'd bought or borrowed from the library. I picked out a book for that day, ambled over to my purple chair, and began to read. If a phone call came in, I'd answer.

"Are you busy?" the caller would ask.

"Yes, I'm working." Sitting in my chair, cats nearby, I was reading a great book. That was my job this year, and it was a good one. The salary was nonexistent, but the satisfaction was daily and deep.

Some mornings after I posted my review I headed out to the local library for a quick cruise of the stacks, looking for new authors or new books by loved authors. I gathered together an armload of books, found a quiet corner with a good chair to sit in, and began reading. '

Westport Public Library has seating scattered throughout its building, but the best spots are the ones beside windows with full views onto the Saugatuck River. On a sunny morning, no matter how cold the temperature outside, I could settle into an illusion of summer heat as I sat there beside a warm window and looked down over a river sparkling and shimmering and dotted with birds. When I closed my eyes against the sun and saw the flashes of yellow and orange against my lids, I was as warm and relaxed as if I were sitting on a desert island, with nothing but a beach chair and my books. Those days I spent in the library I followed the sun around as a flower bends its stem, moving from chair to chair to always be in the light and the warmth.

In my first months of reading, I had always picked my own books, with a gift or two from my mother to add to the bookshelf. Now I had friends—and more friends—offering up books. Handing them over to me with the words, "Read this. I loved it, and I know you will, too."

But what if I didn't love the book? What if I hated it? In the past few months, there had been one or two books, chosen by me, that I'd started and then stopped reading because it had been so clear to me that I didn't like the book and that the book wasn't going to get any better anytime soon. With books given by friends, I didn't have that out. The book was a gift, and gifts were to be read. That is a rule of friendship. And all books read were to be reviewed: that was a rule of my book-a-day year. Therein lay my dilemma. I couldn't just acknowledge the gifted book with a few words, "It was interesting" or "Loved the landscape." I had to write a full and true review.

People share books they love. They want to spread to friends and family the goodness that they felt when reading the book or the ideas they found in the pages. In sharing a loved book, a reader is trying to share the same excitement, pleasure, chills, and thrills of reading that they themselves experienced. Why else share? Sharing a love of books and of one particular book is a good thing. But it is also a tricky maneuver, for both sides. The giver of the book is not exactly ripping open her soul for a free look, but when she hands over the book with the comment that it is one of her favorites, such an admission is very close to the baring of the soul. We are what we love to read, and when we admit to loving a book, we admit that the book represents some aspect of ourselves truly, whether it is that we are suckers for romance or pining for adventure or secretly fascinated by crime.

On the other side of the offered book is the taker. If she is at all a sensitive being, she knows that the soul of the offering friend has been laid wide open and that she, the taker, had better not spit on her friend's soul. I am not exaggerating. Sixteen years ago a friend at work lent me *The Bridges of Madison County* by Robert James Waller. I read the book in one night, and when I discussed it with Mary, I made some comments about how I found the book to be manipulative and unrealistic.

"Sure, I stayed up way too late reading it—I wanted to know if they ever found each other again—but really, that book has nothing to do with how real people carry on. It was romantic nonsense."

Mary told me I'd missed the point entirely, and she stopped

coming by my desk or calling me up for office gossip. By calling her book foolish, I had called her a fool. I would not make that mistake again. But how was I to review a book I didn't like when a friend whom I really liked had given it to me in the first place?

My sisters and I always shared books, from our earliest days as readers through our teens and into adulthood. Natasha and I, horse fanatics both, passed Marguerite Henry books back and forth. My favorite was *Black Gold* and hers was *Misty of Chincoteague*, and we both loved *Born to Trot*. When I turned thirteen, Anne-Marie gave me my own copy of *Steal This Book* by Abbie Hoffman (she knew I'd take her copy from her room and preempted my theft with a gift). I looked through the table of contents. I was interested in all the free stuff, but I was freaked out by references to free abortions and treatment of diseases. What kind of diseases? I had no interest in growing my own marijuana or living in a commune. But the book was a symbol. I closed it and laid it casually on my desk for friends to see when they came over. I had been invited into the world of adults by my older sister. No longer was I the little kid sister; I was moving up.

Anne-Marie gave me my first Wilkie Collins, *The Moonstone*, when I was in law school, thereby beginning an ongoing obsession with him that has never abated in my heart or soul. She also tried to hook me on Anthony Trollope, but I could not get into him or his Barsetshire. When I was laid up in bed for two weeks after a knee operation, she brought me *The Quincunx* by Charles Palliser, a faux Victorian novel complete with a fatherless child, coincidental meetings of great importance, absurd (and wonderful) surnames, and a riveting plot that kept me glued to the book from page 1 through page 781.

The giving of books between sisters offers much less risk of exposure or rejection than between friends. There is both less to hide and less to lose. For one thing, a sister's soul has been bared a few million times before, willingly or not (I did, after all, read Anne-Marie's diary), and for another, my family is always there, come hell or high water. For a friend to offer up a book, much more has been laid on the line. A book offered is an open hand outstretched, taking the chance that it might not be taken, that it might in fact be slapped down. A book offered and a book rejected: Could that ruin a friendship? It had once, with Mary at work, and I didn't want it to happen again.

My friends knew about my book-a-day project, although I tried hard not to talk about it all the time. I didn't want to be the one rhapsodizing through dinner parties about books. I tried not to monopolize all conversations, turning them into book lectures for the benefit of my poor cornered acquaintances. It was bad enough that I was the one singing, "I'm in love, I'm in love, I'm in love, I'm in love, I'm in love with a wonderful book." I was lucky to have more than one chum willing to give me a book and say, "Hey, try this one." I realized that in writing my reviews of such books I could be honest, but I must also be grateful. Grateful for the sharing, for the open soul, and for the friendship.

"Love is blind and that goes for love of books as well," I wrote in my review of *Love Walked In* by Marisa de los Santos. Then I quoted a Flemish expression often used by my mother: *Ieder diertje zijn plez¡ertje*. It literally translates as "Each animal has his pleasure" and means, basically, "To each his own." *Love Walked In* had been a gift, and although the words within the book failed to move me, the giving of the book did move me, profoundly. I knew I was loved with that gift, and that made me feel good. I returned the love with a gift of my own, the lending of *The Third Angel* by Alice Hoffman, a book I'd just read and enjoyed. Did my friend like the lent book? She told me she did, when she returned it a few weeks later.

There are book lovers who never lend out books, for fear of losing their treasures forever. (An old Arab proverb advises, "He who lends a book is an idiot. He who returns the book is more of an idiot.") I have always been a big lender, following Henry Miller's advice: "Like money, books must be kept in constant circulation. Lend and borrow to the maximum—of both books and money! But especially books, for books represent infinitely more than money. A book is not only a friend, it makes friends for you. When you have possessed a book with mind and spirit, you are enriched. But when you pass it on you are enriched threefold." I would make friends with the taking and giving of books, not lose them. If I could not bear parting with a book, especially one in which I'd written notes along the margins and the back pages, I bought an extra copy and handed the new one over.

I came to realize that my acts of reading and sharing, along with my friends' acts of reading and sharing, were being multiplied by readers around the world, as friends and sisters and mothers and sons around the world found books they loved, and shared what they had found with people they loved. The lesson was brought home to me not by the gift of a book but by e-mails. The mother of a good friend e-mailed me from Florida to recommend Garth Stein's *The Art of Racing in the Rain*. A friend in California sent me an e-mail recommending *The White Tiger* by Aravind Adiga: "My book group just read it and some loved it, some hated it. No middle ground." Then a woman from Austria wrote to me to tell me that she'd loved my review of *On Chesil Beach* by Ian McEwan.

"Have you read *Atonement*?" she wrote. "I read it and gave it to everyone I know. Much better than the movie."

My sister-in-law sent me her copy of Hoffman's *Third Angel*. I read it and loved it. It was an easy review to write: "The third angel is when love is unbounded, for just a moment, and that moment is enough to change someone, comfort someone, help someone, save someone. The third angel is what happens when a sunset or a field of heather or a puppy is enough, when love is enough, when just knowing that life's possibilities exist is enough." Or maybe the third angel is when one friend gives a book to another, heart and soul exposed.

I received an e-mail from a man in New York City who had been doing research for a book club meeting and happened upon my review of *The Sin Eater* by Alice Thomas Ellis. Over the next few months he would become a regular correspondent, recommending books like *The Old Man and Me* by Elaine Dundy and *Desperate Characters* by Paula Fox. He and I, complete strangers, made a connection through our love of books. A reader reached out from Germany, the sister of a friend wrote from Brazil with recommendations of Brazilian writers, a woman wrote from Singapore, and I had a whole slew of British book lovers writing in with recommendations. There was a world of voracious readers out there, and they all had "must read" and "loved this" books for me.

There was more to my year of reading than I had first anticipated. Not only was I recovering memories of my own, I was sharing memories of one of life's greatest pleasures, reading, with an ever-larger group of friends and strangers, readers and writers both.

Around the world, on any given day, hundreds, even thousands, of readers might pick up and read the very same book.

There are organized events of shared reading, like the yearly town-wide read led by my local library. One year we read *The Giver* by Lois Lowry; this year we'd be reading *The Housekeeper and the Professor* by Yoko Ogawa. But even without any planning, a woman in California may decide to reread *The Great Gatsby* on the same day a young man in Delhi decides it is time to see if the book beats out the movie, at the same time that a retiree in Warsaw finds a good translation—*Wielki Gatsby*—at a book stall and decides to buy it and begin reading that day.

What do these readers have in common? They might have nothing in common other than knowing how to read and using the skill to enjoy books. I read *Deaf Sentence* by David Lodge in January, and so did many other people, all around the world. I received an e-mail from a woman who lived "in Devon [England] in splendid isolation" who went to hear Lodge do a reading from the novel: it was "fascinating." A woman in Australia wrote to me after reading Paasilinna's *Howling Miller* and later finding my review of it. She suggested I read Bi Feiyu's *Moon Opera*. I lived in suburban Connecticut, she lived outside Melbourne, Paasilinna lived in Finland, and Feiyu lived in China. Around the globe with a book and back again. Each of us brought our own experiences to how we interpreted the book (which in part accounts for the differences in taste in books), but the words we read were the same. We were sharing with each other and with the author.

The benefits of sharing books are "threefold," as Henry Miller promised: a multitude of books to read, a world of new authors to know, and the universe of readers with whom to share the reading experience. The interloper I had feared—books shared from the heart—had instead become a benefit of my year of reading, a bounty to keep me well supplied with new authors, new books, new ideas, and new friends. As old

Aunt Elinor states in Cornelia Funke's *Inkheart*, "Books loved anyone who opened them, they gave you security and friendship and didn't ask anything in return; they never went away, never, not even when you treated them badly. Love, truth, beauty, wisdom and consolation against death. Who had said that? Someone else who loved books." It is this shared love of books and the shared understanding of what they have to offer that holds the world of readers and writers together.

Both sides of the book-lending equation, the giver and the taker, experience fear. How brave we are to overcome that fear to share love, truth, beauty, wisdom, and consolation against death! The threads of friendships entwine over the shared enjoyment of a book. If later a book is shared that is not so mutually enjoyed, the friendship survives. Another day will bring another book, and perhaps another joint experience of connection and satisfaction. I wish I had returned Mary's *Bridges of Madison County* not with a sneer but with a smile, and with another book in hand. Mary had lent me the book around the time I was reading a lot of Laurie Colwin. I could have given her my favorite, *Goodbye Without Leaving*, and said, "Read this. You just might love it."

Friendship saved and book shared.

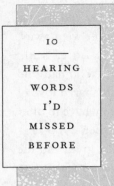

10

———

HEARING

WORDS

I'D

MISSED

BEFORE

Have you ever been heartbroken to finish a book?
Has a writer kept whispering in your ear long after
the last page is turned?

ELIZABETH MAGUIRE,
The Open Door

IN THE SPRING OF ANNE-MARIE'S ILLNESS, I SPENT A SAT-
urday afternoon with her in her study, at her apartment on East
Ninety-sixth Street. She and Marvin had renovated the room
years before, turning a small extra bedroom into an enclosure
of warmth, a cozy office where Anne-Marie could work. A
wide board, the size of a door and painted deep beige, rested
on two short file cabinets in one corner, by a window overlooking Ninety-sixth and Madison. This was Anne-Marie's desk,
adorned that Saturday with stacks of papers, piles of books,
and her laptop, closed now. She hadn't been working in those
last weeks; the pain medication kept her off-kilter, and she was
too tired, all the time. Photos of Marvin were in frames along
the edges of the desk, beside photos of my boys at various ages.
Pictures they had drawn for her were lined up on the wall, resting alongside postcards and Polaroids of places Anne-Marie
had been. Paris. Los Angeles. Fiesole. Pienza. Udaipur. Fire
Island.

The wall opposite the desk housed floor-to-ceiling bookcases, enclosed at the bottom and open on top. The shelves
were jammed with books—art history and philosophy, novels

and poetry, and her collection of Tintin books. The wall between shelves and desk was lined with three windows, northern exposure with muted sunlight. A William Morris print in green and gray papered over the remaining wall space, its vines and flowers overlapping and spreading toward the ceiling.

In the center of the room was a brown couch, fronted by a low coffee table, covered now in books, magazines, and Netflix envelopes. A new addition to the apartment, a television and DVD player, a gift from my parents, faced the couch. Anne-Marie and Marvin had been watching movies at night, waiting for the medication to finally knock my sister out and allow her some hours of sleep before pain and discomfort woke her up again.

Anne-Marie had another visitor that Saturday, a friend from graduate school who taught at Williams College. Liz had come down for a quick visit and left soon after I arrived. She smelled good, a soft perfume of fresh, damp leaves. After she left, her sweet smell lingered, along with the palatable flavor of kindness and concern that now seasoned all visits to my sister. I moved to sit next to Anne-Marie when we were alone, ready to make my usual—and hopefully amusing—report on my "life among the savages." Anne-Marie and I had both loved Shirley Jackson's book of the same name, her hysterically funny account of life in the suburbs with young kids.

But Anne-Marie didn't want to hear about the boys. She turned to me and grabbed hold of me, her skinny arms drawing tight across my back. I buried my face in her hair and listened while she spoke.

"It's not fair," she said.

"I love you," was all I could respond. I burrowed my nose into Anne-Marie's gray sweater and inhaled deeply. It wasn't Liz who had smelled so good. It was Anne-Marie. Of course.

I knew that scent. Mitsouko. Anne-Marie's favorite perfume. I breathed in deep, again and again. I hugged Anne-Marie closer to my rising and lowering chest. I wanted to restore health to her. I wanted to bring back a long life to her future. I could no longer hear what she said to me; I was too close, buried in her hair and sweater.

I have kept the gray sweater. I'm wearing it often these days, feeling the February cold through the windows of my music room, as I sit reading in my purple chair. Upstairs in my closet I keep a half-filled bottle of Mitsouko on a shelf, and when I can bear to, I open it up and breathe in. Sometimes I wonder what words I missed that afternoon, cowering against her shoulder. What wisdom did I fail to hear, or reach for?

In early February, I found words of wisdom in the story of another woman who had died too young. *The Open Door* by Elizabeth Maguire is a fictionalized biography of the nineteenth-century author Constance Fenimore Woolson. The novel begins with a young Woolson rowing out on her own along Mackinac Island in northern Michigan. Woolson is breathing hard as she rows, but she knows it and she likes it, for it is "the gasp of health." She is determined to never get married and suffer the illnesses brought on by childbearing: "It wasn't fair to blame marriage for the deaths of her two sisters, but she wasn't going to risk it. Give up her life for a man? Not her. She had too much to do."

And as Maguire tells the story, Woolson does a lot. She becomes a writer to support herself and her mother, writing short stories, travel pieces, and longer works. She journeys up and down the Eastern Seaboard, and moves her mother south to Florida for her health. She is a voracious reader of all the newest books, and when her mother dies, Woolson heads off to Europe, defying the conventions of mourning, because she is determined to meet one of her literary heroes, Henry James. She and James end up forming a deep and lasting friendship. Woolson never does marry, as she prophesied. She remains independent, relying on romantic interludes with a longtime lover and on friendships such as the one she has with James for companionship.

As I read through *The Open Door*, I found myself liking Woolson more and more. She is enthusiastic about life, strong-willed when it comes to getting what she wants, and she loves books. I underlined again and again the words Maguire puts into Woolson's mouth about the wonder of reading: "Have you ever been heartbroken to finish a book? Has a writer kept whispering in your ear long after the last page is turned?" Yes, yes!

When I was in high school, I began keeping a journal of favorite quotations from books. The purpose of the journal was to act as a vault. I wanted to save the words whispered in my ears by beloved authors, and store them up for the day when I would need to hear them again. As much as they had inspired me when I first read them, I could turn to them when needed and rekindle the inspiration. I hoped back then that by following the words, I would become stronger, wiser, braver, and kinder. The quotes I saved in my journal were the proof of, as well as guidance for, how I would meet any challenge and overcome all difficulties.

Not that I didn't find direction from my parents. But my parents didn't teach us through oft-repeated words of advice or family sayings or long lectures. My father occasionally called us "parasites," like when we asked for a larger allowance or whined about all the weeding and lawn work we had to do, but neither he nor my mother made a big deal about the basic tenets by which they lived. We watched how they behaved, and we learned from their actions.

My parents liked their jobs, and we never heard them complain about having to go to work or putting in long hours (my mother when she was chair of her department at Northwestern, or my father all those nights he was on emergency call). They loved to listen to music, beautiful music like Schubert and Brahms, and the singing of Jacques Brel, Georges Moustaki, and Nana Mouskouri. On Sundays, music was always playing in our house, accompanying us in our long lunches and throughout the lazy afternoon. My parents cared about other people, especially others who, like them, were outsiders in the community. We had frequent dinner guests and overnight visitors, whether newly arrived immigrants, recently hired faculty members, or homesick university students. Our house was open to anyone who needed a little extra support or comfort or just a home-cooked meal.

My father was a surgeon at three hospitals in Chicago, but he also had a family practice in the large Polish neighborhood of Chicago's west side. When patients couldn't pay, my father took promises in lieu of payment and accepted gifts of embroidered pillows, crocheted blankets, and bottles of liquor in thanks for his generosity. He brought the pillows and blankets home, and left the vodka in the office. One afternoon while at work, my father heard an explosion from the storage room. Four bottles of home-brewed vodka had exploded, leaving headache-inducing fumes in the air and shards of glass everywhere.

One of my very first memories from childhood is of being taken on an Open Housing march by my mother. It was the fall of 1966, and I had just turned four years old. That summer, Martin Luther King Jr. had started his Freedom Movement in Chicago to open up white neighborhoods to black families. Organizers from Evanston began their own campaign to integrate our town's neighborhoods, staging long walks that began in the predominantly black part of town and then passed through the almost exclusively white areas.

My parents had had firsthand experience with segregated housing. In 1964 they bought a house in a small development on the border of Evanston and Skokie. Soon after moving in, they discovered a covenant in the deed of the house that had never been pointed out to them by their lawyer or by the lawyer of the couple who sold them the house. The deed prohibited the selling of any house in our cul-de-sac to a "non-Caucasian." My parents were outraged, and they, along with a few other families on the street, drew up a petition to remove the clause from the deed.

My mother walked through the neighborhood, asking for signatures to the petition. Doors were slammed in her face, and nasty notes were left in our mailbox. Anne-Marie and Natasha were told by local kids, "We can't play with you anymore," while their parents sued my parents for harassment (the suit was later dropped). My family finally moved out of the cul-de-sac and into a house with no restrictive covenants.

My mother began attending the Open Housing meetings held at Evanston's Ebenezer AME Church. When the marches were organized, she went along, taking us with her. The marches always began with a sermon in the brick church, people packed tightly into its small interior. After the sermon, we spilled out of the church in waves. I remember feeling suddenly cold after the heat of the church and looking up to see hundreds of stars in the sky. Everyone was excited. There was a lot of laughing and singing. For me, it felt like a holiday, and I clapped along. The campaign leaders set us up in a long snaking line and led us in singing "We Shall Overcome." My mother placed me in a stroller for the long walk ahead, and with my sisters at her side, we moved forward with the crowd.

As strong as my parents' examples were, I remember as a kid wanting to hear some words of advice from them. I clung to the words my father spoke once, when my sisters and I were complaining about something—"Do not look for happiness in life. Life itself is happiness."—and I wanted more. I remembered the sermons we listened to in the Ebenezer Church before heading out on our marches, especially when the pastor quoted verbatim from Martin Luther King, urging us all to "open the doors of opportunity to everyone, all of God's Children. . . . We have to let justice roll down like water and let righteousness flow like a mighty stream." At four years old, how could I know what those words meant? Somehow, I did.

In the books I read as a kid, parents gave out advice, or if not parents, some kind of authority figure did. Ole Golly in *Harriet the Spy* was always quoting Dostoyevsky, Cowper, Emerson, and Shakespeare while advising Harriet on how to live her life. But my parents were not that way. They lived according to their own principles, and expected us to follow along, or not. How or if we followed along, and all the big and little decisions, were left to us to decide.

Not all my decisions were good ones. I smoked in high school and drank, pilfering bottles of Chivas from the basement, gifts to my father that he didn't keep track of. I wasn't drunk the night I hit a police car and ran from the scene of the accident. I was completely sober that evening, and just trying to help out a friend whose car was blocked by another car at a party. He had to get home, and having noticed that the keys of the blocking car were in its ignition, I offered to move it out of the way. No matter that I was fifteen and had been in driver's ed for only two weeks. I jumped in, turned the key, and backed down the driveway, never looking behind me. I will never forget the sound of the crash or the sudden jolt of impact. I got out of the car, saw the smashed-up front of a black-and-white police cruiser, and took off running. I ran through yards, and then went up and over a high fence. I fell down hard onto the other side, twisting my ankle. Hobbling all the way, I made it home to find the police already there, waiting. I had to sit in the back of the police car all by myself, while my parents followed behind in their car.

Other than spending a terrifying night in the police station, I got off easy. When my court date came, no police officers showed up to testify against me, and all charges were dropped. The punishment I received from my parents was fair: I was grounded for six weeks. The punishment I got at school was worse. I was teased, and kids I didn't know pointed at me and sniggered. Friends dropped me when they realized I could no longer go out after school or on the weekends, or because their parents advised them against hanging out with me. A few loyal friends stuck close, and my sister Natasha stayed in nights to keep me company. Anne-Marie was already off at college, and she thought the whole incident was hilarious. Looking back now, I realize how lucky I was that I didn't hurt anybody, and I can see that the weekends spent at home cured my too-early habits of smoking and drinking. At the time, I remember turning to my book of quotations. I used the words I found there to shore myself up and get through the mess I'd made.

I still have that high school journal of favorite quotes. The mix of obvious and obscure lines reflects my adolescent mind's struggle for answers. There are two lines from *A Separate Peace* by John Knowles: "An arrogant determination to live had not yet given out," and "Only Phineas never was afraid, only Phineas never hated anyone." I walked through the school hallways after my traffic accident, head held high,

repeating under my breath, "never afraid, never hated anyone. . . ." From Margaret Mitchell's *Gone with the Wind* I'd
copied "After all, tomorrow is another day," and this one also
I recited in my head, walking along. At night before going to
sleep, I reread more quotes I'd penned in, like Dickens's great
line from *A Tale of Two Cities*: "It is a far, far better thing that
I do, than I have ever done" (Backing a car into a cop car and
running away? Hardly!); and the quote I'd copied out in great,
sweeping letters, "People do not complete us, we complete ourselves," taken from *The Second Sex* by Simone de Beauvoir.

I needed words again. I needed guidance from books. Yes,
I still wanted to follow Knowles's "arrogant determination to
live," but the "how" of living needed bolstering and fattening
and enriching. I had to reopen and restock my vault of wisdom.
I needed again to hear from authors about their experiences. In
reading about experiences both light and dark, I would find the
wisdom to get through my own dark times.

According to the historical evidence, Constance Fenimore
Woolson either jumped or fell to her death at the age of fifty-
three, suffering from influenza and depression. But Maguire
imagines a different ending for her character. She has Woolson discovering that she has a tumor in her head, and that she
has only months left to live. Maguire herself became ill with
ovarian cancer while writing *The Open Door* and finished the
novel during the final months of her life, before she died at age
forty-seven. Did Maguire write her ending so that Woolson's
character could serve as the voice for Maguire's own fears
about death and eventual acceptance of what was coming? I am
certain that it is Maguire talking when she has Woolson say,
"Hard to believe, but once I had absorbed the shock, a certain
giddiness followed. Suddenly I had a reprieve from the minor

oppressions of everyday life. . . . It was like having a pass to be one's most selfish and unsocial self."

As a storyteller herself, Maguire channels the storyteller in Woolson to relate her own struggles: "Storytellers live in the future tense. All my life I had pulled myself out of low spirits by imagining what might happen next. Now there was not going to be any next. Everything needed to be experienced as it was. This was a test of my pragmatic soul." Her words exalt the desire of living on through her words, through readers' witnessing of her own experience: "Gone . . . it is impossible to conceive of oneself as gone, isn't it? . . . In my imagination, I was still there, watching from the heavens. . . . It seems I am just a small hole dug in the sand by a child's shovel, to be erased with the next turn of the tide. I would rather be a mountain, to stand purple and glorious for all time."

I use the words of Maguire, imagined for Woolson, as a proxy for the lost murmurings of Anne-Marie, and to fill in all that was left unsaid between us that afternoon in her study. I put myself back on the brown couch, my arms close around my sister, and smell again the damp, fresh leaves of her perfume. I hear the words Maguire wrote, and I find comfort. When I return to my purple chair, the low winter sun outside my window and fat cat in my lap, I reach to touch the sleeves of the gray sweater I'm wearing. Anne-Marie is "still there, watching from the heavens."

How I wish I could get the message to Maguire—*Your words have whispered to me!*—and let her know that she indeed created a "mountain, standing glorious for all time," a mountain for me. A mountain made up of words, and offering wisdom. Through the door she opened between us, Maguire counsels me that life is precious and fragile. She advises me to live like her wonderful character Woolson, with spirit and intelligence and bravado. She comforts me that while death is scary, it is also inevitable, for all of us, and that if she could face it head-on, Anne-Marie could too.

Maguire used Woolson as a guide and a cipher. Now I would use both women. Four months into my year of reading, and their words found me. They whisper to me and urge me on. I've packed the quotes into my vault, to carry along with me, and to return to again and again.

11

———

WHERE

WARMTH

IS

FOUND

"Nothing don't matter," he said, looking up at the ceiling but not seeing the ceiling.
"It matter to me, Jefferson," she said. "You matter to me."

ERNEST J. GAINES,
A Lesson Before Dying

I'M ALWAYS COLDEST IN THE LAST WEEKS OF WINTER. MY body is worn out from keeping itself warm for months, and I can no longer fight against the chills coming in under the door. In an effort to find sun and warmth, I read *Scat* by Carl Hiaasen on the last day of February. I knew Hiaasen would take me to Florida, immerse me in heat and humidity, and make me want to live out of a canoe, traveling around the sprawling wildernesses of southern Florida's Ten Thousand Islands. I had a great trip, but when I rose from my purple chair, the grass outside my window was still brown. Snow survived in dirty clumps, glistening wet and icy under a cold gray sky. I wasn't in Florida anymore. I was in a Connecticut winter, and it was ugly.

I went to my computer to read over again the Facebook message I'd received just days before. It was from Andrew. Twenty-seven years ago I'd promised to love Andrew forever. A month ago he'd lobbed a friend request my way, and I'd accepted. Friendship I could renew. But love? When I made my promise of undying devotion all those years ago, the promise was more like a threat: he was breaking up with me, and I swore I'd never forget him. "And you'll never forget me," was my final curse.

I fell in love for the first time when I was away at horseback-riding camp. I was twelve, and so was Tim, a kid from Milwaukee. We worshipped the ground each other rode on. After the four weeks of camp were over, we never saw each other again, but I liked thinking about him for months afterward.

My next bout of love was with a boy I met in Seville, Spain, when I was seventeen years old. I was in town for ten days with a group from my high school, and I met him on my first day there. He was a friend of the girl with whom I was staying. Alicia was a nice girl but a little wild, with heavily lined eyes, deeply painted lips, and a pack of cigarettes always sticking out from her back pocket. Her father was a strict man, a professor and a conservative Catholic, but he just adored his daughter. As long as she got good grades, she explained to me, he let her do pretty much as she pleased. And it pleased her to go out with her boyfriend late at night and stay out until early in the morning. Our first night out together, the two of them introduced me to Alfonso.

Alfonso was handsome, with curved lips and big brown eyes. He had a straight nose, perfect cheekbones, and a dimple when he smiled. He was a little unkempt, with greasy hair, pants that hung down from a notched-up leather belt, and a shirt that rose off his back when he leaned forward to shake my hand. He was polite and gracious and not a bit confident. He made me feel comfortable. We hung out in the local bar that first night, drinking beer, and then left for one of Seville's public parks. While Alicia and her boyfriend kissed on the bench beside us, Alfonso and I muddled on in conversation, his English just a little bit better than my Spanish.

Alfonso loved his city, and he told me all about her. Seville had been a Muslim capital for hundreds of years, he explained, which accounted for the Moorish architecture everywhere. Then Ferdinand III, the Catholic king from the north of Spain, came along and ran all the Muslims out. He moved himself into the Alcazar, the former Muslim palace.

"You must visit it. It is so beautiful." Alfonso took my hand and went on talking.

The Cathedral of Saint Mary of the See in Seville was built on the site of the former mosque of the long-gone Muslim rulers. Beside the cathedral is the Giralda, a tower originally built as a minaret. Instead of stairs, the tower had ramps inside, allowing Muslim muezzins to ride to the top on horseback.

Alfonso told me the Sevillan motto, *"No me ha dejado,"* explaining that it meant Seville would never abandon her people.

"And I will never abandon Seville," he promised, holding tighter onto my hand and looking soulfully into my eyes. I was hooked.

For the next six days, Alfonso and I spent every afternoon and evening together. *Semana Santa* (Holy Week), traditionally a week for Catholics to make final penance before Easter, had begun. The days were marked by long processions of men wearing white robes and hoods walking behind floats carrying painted polychrome Madonnas. The men were called *nazarenos*, and they bore large wooden crosses across their backs to commemorate the sufferings of Jesus Christ. Onlookers cheered the men on and attached money, trinkets, and flowers to the floats, following the procession to the end with singing and wailing.

When the parades ended, it was time to hit the bars. A favorite drink of the holiday was the *postura*, a mixture of gin and white wine. I liked the crisp taste of the drink, the way it hit the back of my throat and then slid down, a slither of fire down to my belly. The bars were packed with people, and the smell of sawdust from the floor mixed in with the smoke from Ducados and Marlboros. For a girl from the Midwest, this was life straight out of *Carmen*, brought to modern times, and with my own handsome bullfighter beside me. We made out in the dark corners of packed bars and fed each other off tiny plates of fresh shrimp, garlicky potato tortillas, and meaty green olives.

One day toward the end of the week it was Alfonso's turn to carry a heavy wooden cross down the streets of Seville. I couldn't tell which of the hooded men he was, so I just cheered on everyone who passed. The next day Alfonso took me home to meet his parents. He lived in a huge stone house off a quiet square of orange trees and yellow cobblestones. We sat in a room with ceilings fifteen feet high and walls lined with patterned wallpaper. Heavy, dark portraits hung around us, and we sat in ornate wooden chairs just like the ones I would see ten years later in the furnished rooms at the Metropolitan Museum of Art. The parents spoke English beautifully and offered me orange soda to drink and almond cookies to eat. Suddenly the mother of Alfonso leaned over to take a closer look at her son. A closer look at his neck. The same neck I'd been passionately biting less than eight hours earlier.

"*Hijo!* Your neck has many bruises!"

I sank into the cushions of my eighteenth-century chair.

"It's from carrying the cross, Mama."

"You're a good boy," she said, sitting back again with a smile.

I was hit by a car the next morning. I was crossing the street to go home after a long night, and I never saw the car coming. I refused to take the accident as a sign of divine retribution, payback for the lie we'd perpetrated on Alfonso's mother. Even later, when the distraught driver brought me a present in the hospital, a light-up version of La Giralda, and it blew up in my face as I plugged it in, I refused to see God's hand in my plight. All I could see was Alfonso. I was in love.

The day I left Seville, the father of my host family wished me luck with Alfonso and advised me to hold on to him.

"He comes from an old Sevillan family on his father's side. And on his mother's side, there is Franco."

I had fallen in love with a boy from the family of Francisco Franco. Alfonso was all lover and no fighter, but the thought of Franco made me shiver in my sandals.

I wasn't able to hold on to Alfonso—time and distance took care of that. I did see him again, three years later, when I was back in Spain for my junior year of college. He was living outside London, and I visited him there. He took me out for a curry in Tunbridge Wells. He was still the sweet boy he'd been in Seville, and as handsome as ever in his own disheveled way. I was no longer in love, but I loved how nice he had been to me, and I loved remembering our walks through the crowded streets of Seville at all hours of the night, the glasses of *postura* we shared, and how he talked about the city while holding tightly on to my hand.

I fell in love a few more times over the years, and thought each and every man was the love of my life. As Nancy Mitford has her character "the Bolter" say in *The Pursuit of Love*, "One always thinks that, every time." The Bolter would know: she left her children time and time again to pursue new loves. I'd married the last love of my life, and we were happy. Now out of the blue, a man for whom I'd written volumes of poetry and crossed campus six times in one night for one more good-night kiss, and on whose chest I'd written my name in Sharpie to keep other women away, wanted back into my life. I had good memories of our times together, but love?

Back in December, I'd read *Twilight* at the urging of a friend's daughter, and I found it hilarious. Thinking now about love, I saw how adept Stephenie Meyer was at portraying that first thrill of wanting more, physically and soulfully, from another person. Bella, teenage girl and the new kid at school, is lonely and feeling like a misfit. She finds herself strangely attracted to Edward, her handsome, sexy, well-dressed, and very smart lab partner. When she finds out he is a vampire, her desire doesn't diminish. If anything, it grows. Bella describes her "overpowering craving to touch" her beloved vampire, and I recognized that sensation. I'd felt it in Seville for the first time, and it was scary but wonderful. There is no thrill like the anticipation of that first kiss. Meyer cleverly entwines teen hormones (sexual desire) and unexplainable phenomena (vampires) and twists sexual longing into a battle between good and evil. Desire is a monster, but a monster that the young lover (goodness) will accept and encourage because she is so sure the evil within desire can be tamed. Alfonso had no evil in him, but Andrew certainly did, and the desire to tame him had been irresistible twenty-seven years ago.

Maybe that is what love is: the taming of desire into something solid and sustainable. The passion I share with Jack is different from our first New Year's Eve kiss twenty years ago. Weeks after that first spark of desire, Jack flew off on a business trip. I couldn't bear the time away from him, and I jumped on a plane to meet him in Utah. We watched a lightning storm over Salt Lake City and spent the weekend at the Snowed Inn, up in the Park City hills. These days our passion is more content to stay at home, manifesting itself through affection, proffered cups of coffee, and whatever time alone we can wrest away from kids, his work, and my reading. We still have our *Twilight* moments, but even better, we have a love that has lasted more than twenty years.

In *Family Happiness* by Laurie Colwin, a woman with a perfect life, including husband, job, kids, and plenty of money and leisure time, falls in love with another man. Her husband and her kids are not enough for her. She explains that love in the family is "intelligent and deep, and never unrequited. It was the basis of all good things and there was nothing secret or covert about it." On the other hand, her private love, the desire she has for the man outside of her family, is "feckless, led to nothing, was productive of nothing, and didn't do anyone a bit of good." Because *Family Happiness* is more fantasy than fact, Polly keeps both kinds of love in her life, the one of desire and passion and the enduring love of family. No one ever finds out about her lover, no one ever gets hurt, and only Polly has to suffer "a life of conflict and pain," a price she deems well worth it.

In Ford Madox Ford's novel *The Good Soldier*, love is given harsh treatment. Two couples, duplicitous and needy, manipulate desire as a weapon on the battlefield of life. When love manifests itself, suddenly and unexpectedly, it is seen as a weakness but also as a threat that must be squashed by the other characters through "perfectly normal, virtuous, slightly deceitful" activity. Desire can be indulged, but in Ford's book, love leads only to madness and suicide.

In Maggie Estep's *Alice Fantastic*, falling in love is simple, necessary, and basic. What happens *after* falling in love is more complicated, with plenty of desire, dependence, and jealousy expressed, fought against, and finally accepted. This loving was a vibe I understood, love not as a battlefield but as a series of leaps into the unknown, with an occasional bump, the rare injury, and a high-flying exhilaration that makes the bumps and injuries worth it.

Alice Fantastic offers all varieties of romantic love, but what had me rooted to the book is Estep's portrayal of the love between the two sisters, Alice and Eloise. The sisters have grating differences and opposing outlooks on everything from work to romance. When they discover that they have unknowingly shared a lover (through individually experienced one-night stands), the accidental couplings only underscore their differences. Eloise feels cheap and angry, and Alice feels fine, although she'll never sleep with William again.

When facing up to the secret revealed about their mother, the two sisters finally join together: "The tears came and Alice wrapped me in her arms and held me for a long, long time. We were like little kids then. The oceans of differences calm." The "oceans of differences" between them are nothing compared to the love. The only thing they have in common (other than an accidental lover and a love of dogs) is how for each of them the person they love most, along with their mother, is the other.

It is only within the sibling relationship that such a dichotomy exists. I loved my sisters even when I might never have befriended them across a cafeteria table or at a party. I have more in common with my parents than I used to feel comfortable admitting to, but I had very little in common with Anne-Marie, other than our love for books and for beauty in art. Natasha and I have interests more in sync, yet none of us three sisters had similar friends or lovers. None of us could ever agree on the ideal meal, vacation, house, or political platform. When I started having kids, our disagreements extended to names, haircuts, and bedtimes for a child. As Rilke writes in his poem "The Sisters," "Look how the same possibilities / unfold in their opposite demeanors." And yet we loved each other completely and without question. We were there in the most important moments, and in the smaller ones too.

Anne-Marie was the first of my family to meet Jack. Her

animated approval ("You two are like twins, perfect together!") went a long way with everyone, me included. She
walked me through my first labor pains with Peter. Up and
down along the Hudson River we paced, Anne-Marie keeping
track of the time of each contraction on a piece of paper. Every birthday that followed, Peter got a home-baked cake from
her. The best cake was the Lego brick–shaped one, frosted in
bright red. I have a photo album of all the cakes she made over
the years. In every photo she is leaning toward Peter with a big
smile, her baked confection offered with both hands.

The simplest and yet profoundly moving explanation of
love came to me through the words of a character in Ernest
J. Gaines's *A Lesson Before Dying*. The novel tells the story of
Grant, a young man from the South who, having studied to become a teacher, is roped into visiting Jefferson, a boy sentenced
to death row for a murder he witnessed but did not commit. Jefferson's godmother wants Grant to offer Jefferson a modicum
of education before he dies, so that he can die like a man, and
not like the "hog" his own defense attorney called him. She
wants to give her godson the dignity in the end to know "that
he did not crawl to that white man, that he stood at that last moment and walked."

During a visit to the prison, Grant witnesses Jefferson saying to his godmother, "It don't matter. . . . Nothing don't matter." His godmother answers, "It matter to me, Jefferson. . . .
You matter to me."

You matter to me. Reading those words, I thought my heart
would burst. That is the crux of love, one person mattering to
another person, one existence that is important among all other
lives. One person can count for something individual and special. We are not interchangeable. We are unique in how we are
loved.

Desire for a person is not the same thing as having that unique appreciation and need for them, nor is affection. Desire waxes and wanes, and affection can be felt without long-standing commitment. But "You matter to me" means that the long haul is accepted, even willingly taken on: I will carry you, hold you, and applaud you, from here on in. Dependability: I will be here to take care of you. And when you are gone, I will be here to remember you.

A few days before the sudden Facebook message from Andrew, I had gotten a call from Jack. The boys were all home from school and I was just finishing up my book for the day, *The Age of Dreaming* by Nina Revoyr.

"Meet me at the doctor's office. I'm having chest pains." One hour later I watched him being taken away on a stretcher, hooked up to monitors and oxygen and God knows what else. I went home to tell the boys nothing, just that I was leaving early for my Improv class and that Peter was in charge of ordering pizza and getting everyone to bed on time. I kissed them all and left for the hospital.

The man at admissions sent me to the cardiac care unit with a wink: "Let me know if things don't work out." He was hitting on a potential widow? My skin crawled. Tears, held back so far, now came streaming down my cheeks.

Jack, as it turned out, would be fine. I would not be a widow, bad luck for the admissions Romeo. Jack had not suffered a heart attack. All the tests showed normal heart activity, good oxygen levels, and sound health. I spent the evening by his side, reassuring myself that he was okay. By the time the doctor came in for his evening summation, I was more concerned with going out into a dark and desolate parking lot than I was with the health of my husband. We were meant to have many more years together: we *both* had to stay alive. The doctor assured me that the lot was monitored, but he was willing to walk me to my car.

"No, I'll stay just a bit longer," I answered and returned to holding on to Jack's hand. The last love of my life: I was holding on for as many years as we had together.

My father's first and last love is my mother. He met her at an evening lecture of a philosophy class at the University of Leuven. He'd started medical school there, and she was a literature student. While the professor at the front of the lecture hall went on about Saint Thomas Aquinas, my father sketched my mother's picture into his notebook. He still has that sketch, the notebook kept safe in a drawer by his bed. My mother had plenty of suitors before my father, but never fell in love. Her first marriage proposal was offered by the boy's mother. He himself was too shy to ask. When my mother refused the offer, the shy boy ran off to the French Foreign Legion. As far as I know, no old boyfriends popped up in my mother's life once my parents moved to America, but then her generation didn't have Facebook to deal with.

It isn't Facebook that brings old lovers face-to-face in Nicole Krauss's book *The History of Love*. It is perseverance. The novel is the story of Leo: he "was a great writer. He fell in love. It was his life." Writing and loving. But war separates him from his first lover, Alma, and she finds a new man, thinking she has lost Leo forever. When Leo finds Alma again, years later, what can she do? She holds on to the words he has written for her— he is a writer, after all—but she tells him to go. He continues to love her, but she loves only the memories she has of him.

Loving my memories of Andrew was not the same thing as loving Andrew. With Alfonso I had even sweeter memories— he never dumped me—but I didn't love him either. The truth was that no matter how good the memories, those guys just had not been there for the long haul. I did not share thousands of moments with them, and there was nothing enduring about my long-ago feelings for them. I had nostalgia for those feelings but I no longer felt them. I had my answer to the question lurking in a Facebook message: *I loved you once, but not still.*

"Nothing in the world matters except Love," an old friend gushes to the narrator of *The Provincial Lady in London* by E. M. Delafield. Her response? "A banking account, sound teeth, and adequate servants matter a great deal more." I laughed and underlined the words. And suddenly I was reminded of the words used by Jefferson's godmother in *A Lesson Before Dying*: "You matter to me." It is not the emotion of love, solely and independent, that is important. It is the *people* I love who hold the word steady for me.

Of course there are plenty of little things that do matter in life, like a bank account and sound teeth, and plenty of things that don't matter at all, like the state of my hair or the dust bunnies burrowing under every bed in the house. But amid all the big and the little stuff, the cardiac unit and the Facebook messages and the dust, it is the people I love that matter most of all.

I should let them know just how much they matter, at all times, to me. Words of love will keep us warm, even through the last days of winter.

12

———

THE
EXPANSION
OF
EXPERIENCE

Now that I had taken the pains to learn something about it, I had better ask if I really wanted to know. I did. I needed to know, but I am not glad to know.

WENDELL BERRY,
Hannah Coulter

ON THE NIGHT OF FEBRUARY 13, 1945, MY FATHER SAW flames and smoke rising from Dresden, five miles off in the distance. Through the dark hours of the night and into the dawning of the next day, he watched in disbelief, his stomach in a knot, as the city was firebombed. He could smell the smoke and he knew there were more than buildings burning. He'd been on the road with thousands and thousands of refugees fleeing the incoming Soviet army. While he had camped in a field, the refugees continued on into Dresden, to join the citizens of one of Europe's most beautiful cities and thousands more refugees.

By the time the bombing was over, Dresden was destroyed and most of its people killed, incinerated or suffocated in their underground bunkers. Estimates of the number of people who died in the two days of bombing range from tens of thousands to hundreds of thousands. My father could have been one of those people if he had not stopped to rest and sleep in a field. My father could have been killed two years earlier when the partisans came to the family farmhouse and killed Sergei, Antonina, and Boris. He lived through the war, or else I wouldn't be reading these books now. But living, like dying, caused ripples to spread through his life, impacts from what he saw, what he suffered, what he knew.

When I began my year of reading, a cousin from Belgium sent me a book titled *The Assault*, written by Dutch author Harry Mulisch. For months it sat on my bookshelf, relegated to a far corner. "But it is a great book," my cousin insisted. He didn't understand that I was frightened by the book's cover photograph of a dead body lying on a street, and even more by the text on the back cover: "A Nazi collaborator, infamous for his cruelty, is assassinated. . . . The Germans retaliate by slaughtering an innocent family." I was scared to read the book because I knew it was about war and revenge and hate. I had heard the stories from my father, and I knew what had happened during the war. Did I really want to read about it?

But finally, in late March, I went over to the shelf and pulled the book down. It was my year to experience whatever great books had to share with me, and my own fears couldn't stand in the way.

When I began to read *The Assault*, I did not get up again for three hours. Weaving a story around an actual event, the novel is about the murder of a cruel Dutch policeman during the final days of the Nazi occupation of the Netherlands and how that one murder had a lasting impact on everyone involved, from the family wrongly blamed for the murder to the German officers who responded with swift and horrible retaliation to the actual killers, as well as to the family of the slain officer.

At the beginning of the novel, a boy named Anton walks beside a canal, fascinated by the waves caused by a passing motorboat: "All across the water a complicated braiding of ripples developed which went on changing for several minutes. . . . Each time Anton tried to figure out exactly how this happened, but each time the pattern became so complex that he could no longer follow it." As I read further into the book, I realized that this "complicated braiding of ripples" was a premonition of what was coming, the murder of the police officer and the subsequent killing of everyone in Anton's family except for the boy himself. Anton will spend the rest of his life trying to untangle the events of that night of horror, struggling to understand why the Dutch officer was killed, why his family was targeted for vengeance, and where in the puzzle of pain the rest of the players fit.

After the war ends, Anton is taken in by relatives and goes back to school, eventually building a career and falling in love. Moments of happiness and even joy reemerge over his lifetime, as when he has a son, whom he names for his dead brother Peter. But still Anton searches for the full story of that one night, wondering why he survived and his family did not. Survival itself is a "complicated braiding of ripples," the consequences of war being scars of loss and fear, anger and bewilderment. For Anton, the scars of war are his abiding pessimism and the haunting memory of that horrible night outside his house: "The world is hell. . . . Even if we had heaven on earth tomorrow, it couldn't be perfect because of all that's happened. Never again could things be set right."

For my father, the consequences of war brought him far from home, and eventually across an ocean, to start over in a new world. My parents tell me I was named after the members of the corps de ballet of the Bolshoi, most of whom were named Nina. They went to see a performance of the Bolshoi just days before I was born. But I also know that my name is another ripple effect of the war, coming from my father's sister Antonina, who was murdered that night in 1943. Much as Anton took the name of his dead brother for his own son, my name is a remembrance of a life lost, of a sibling taken away.

The final chapter of *The Assault* finds Anton, now middle-aged, being swept up in an antinuclear rally. The protesters march against a future war, the war of mutual nuclear destruction. But Anton is not optimistic that a nuclear battle can be stopped. He believes that "everything is forgotten in the end," and he doesn't mean forgotten as in forgiven, but forgotten as in no lessons learned. He believes the experience of war, in all its horrors, is doomed to be repeated over and over.

Reading in my purple chair, I shrank from Anton's conclusion. Is everything forgotten in the end? Are no lessons ever learned? I thought back to the first book I ever read about war, *Across Five Aprils* by Irene Hunt. *Across Five Aprils* tells the story of the Creighton family from southern Illinois. The family is divided by the Civil War when one brother joins up with the Union army and another son goes south to fight with the Confederacy.

I read the book in 1975, as part of my curriculum in middle school. Our country was coming out of the Vietnam War then, and yet our teacher failed to make the connection between what we were reading, with its descriptions of battles and injuries, families torn apart by war, and a country ravaged by dissension, and what we ourselves were living through. As eighth-graders born in 1962, our entire lives had played out under the shadow of the Vietnam War. We were ready to discuss the parallels between the conflicts of the 1860s and the conflicts of the 1960s and '70s. We would have welcomed the chance to talk about war and make sense of it—or not. Instead our teacher taught *Across Five Aprils* as a historically placed novel that mirrored facts we were learning in social studies, facts we had to learn about for a test and could then forget.

I remember going to church on a Sunday in the early 1970s, a few years before I would read *Across Five Aprils*. The priest gave a sermon condemning all the protests against the war in Vietnam.

"We must give unwavering support to our nation's war against communism and godlessness. I say to you, America, love it or leave it."

My mother tensed in the pew beside me, her breath suddenly sharp and ragged. When the service ended, she marched out of that church with her jaw trembling and her arms swinging. I don't remember how she began her haranguing of the priest, but I do remember standing beside her on the sidewalk outside the church and hearing the rise and fall of her voice, how it choked with anger and then tears. I held on to her skirt and felt the swell of her conviction.

"Democracy depends on the voices of its citizens, whether supportive or critical of the government! Leave America? No, I choose to try and make it a better country. A country that ends wars, not perpetuates them."

I felt her outrage that a man of God extolled the waging of war. As Kurt Vonnegut once said, describing his own World War II experiences, "War is murder," and we better not forget it. The priest at Saint Athanasius had forgotten. My mother hadn't forgotten, nor had my father. We never went back to that church again.

I often find myself at dinner parties arguing over the altruism of human beings. One dinner stands out in my memory, a meal of lobster alongside a pool in East Hampton on a warm summer evening. At a table of eight, I found myself the only one willing to believe that humans are inherently cooperative and productive. I looked around the table at my dinner mates, all products of loving families, solid public educations, and open career opportunities. How could they not grasp that it was the goodness of humanity upon which all of their bounty was based? I laid claim to the fine meal, long-held friendships, and burgeoning families (babies were in tow) as proof of the big and small feats of goodness and selflessness that humans are capable of. But one of the women at the table raised what is always believed to be the trump card in any argument over mankind's goodness:

"What about war? If we're so good, why do we go out and kill each other?"

I couldn't answer Liza. But now I know what I should have told her.

"Read a book," I should have said, "to find out why we go to war, to experience what it is that drives us to violence."

We weren't going to resolve the question of mankind's inherent goodness or evil sitting out on a deck on a summer night. But maybe, just maybe, if Liza took a book to bed and read it, really read it, she'd come closer to understanding our own closeted selves, our ambitions and our desires. And the impact that those desires have on our lives, for good and for bad.

The main character in Wendell Berry's *Hannah Coulter* turns to books to understand war. Her first husband goes off to Europe in 1942 and is killed. Hannah marries again, and her second husband, Nathan, is drafted and sent to the Pacific theater. He comes back home having fought in the battle of Okinawa. He never talks to Hannah or anybody else about what he saw there. When he dies, decades later, Hannah finds herself filled with an urgent need to know about the battle, and she looks for answers in books: "I needed to know, but I am not glad to know."

What she finds out through her reading is that the horrors her husband lived through are unavoidable facts of war. War is "a human storm of explosions and quakes and fires, a man-made natural disaster gathering itself up over a long time out of ignorance and hatred, greed and pride, selfishness and a silly love of power . . . passing like a wind-driven fire over the quiet land and kind people." Hannah tracks back the consequences of war not only for her husband, but for herself and for their children. She needs to know what his experience of war was to understand how he acted later, as both husband and father. She comes to see that he needed the quiet of their hometown and the encircling of their family and her love to keep his knowledge of war at bay: "He needed to know that he was here and I was here with him, that he had come back from the world of war, again, to this. Reassured, he would sleep again, and I too would sleep."

Books are the weapon against Anton's lament that "everything is forgotten in the end." Books allow experiences to be relived, and allow lessons to be learned. Anton's frustration in watching the ripples left on a canal by a passing barge and not being able to "figure out exactly how it happened" is not my frustration. I understood the ripples and their impacts because *The Assault* traces back and exposes the links between that one horrible night and the lives of everyone there. Having read the book, I can imagine and I will never forget the costs of war. I have experienced what Anton experienced, and now I will always remember him.

By reading *The Assault* and *Hannah Coulter*, I experienced— safely, yes, but still with sweat and with tears—war. Just as in other books, like *Alice Fantastic* and *Family Happiness*, I had experienced love and lust. The difference was that I had shied away from reading books about war, from having an experience that was scary and jarring and upsetting. And now I understood why it was important to read these books. Because being witness to all types of human experience is important to understanding the world, but also to understanding myself. To define what is important to me, and who is important, and why.

For Anton, war was proof of man's inherent violence. For Nathan, Hannah Coulter's second husband, that proof was tempered by what he knew of his own family, and of his own quiet place in the universe. My father, like Anton, suffered the loss of family during a murderous act of war. But he did not carry from his experience of war an abiding pessimism about the nature of mankind. He was more like Nathan, both in having witnessed war's devastation and in how he turned inward after the war, building an existence of family and work that protected him. As Hannah describes it, "Our life in our place had been a benediction to him, but he had seen it always within a circle of fire that might have closed upon it."

I was, along with my mother and my sisters, my father's shield against the past, a buffer zone between him and the pain he'd known. And even more than a protection, we were a promise of better things to come. Now that Anne-Marie had died, there was a rent in the shield, a rift in the buffer, a breaking of the promise. I could patch over the hole, but the bump of repair would always be there, a rough and uneven space marking her absence. As for the promise, I was doing what I could to recover it for everyone in my family. I was reading.

And in reading, I discovered that the burden of living is the uneven and unlimited allotment of pain. Tragedy is conferred randomly and unfairly. Any promise of easy times to come is a false one. But I know I can survive the hard times, taking the worst of what happens to me as a burden but not as a noose. Books mirrored life—my life! And now I understood that all the bad and sad stuff that happens to me, and that happened to the people I was reading about, is both the cost and the proof of resilience.

The value of experience, real or imagined, is that it shows us how to—or how *not* to—live. In reading about different characters and the consequences of their choices, I was finding myself changed. I was discovering new and distinct ways of undergoing life's sorrows and joys. I could follow the example of my father, and hold my family closely around me, or I could pattern myself after Anton, and turn sour and dark over the nature of the world. I chose my father's way.

The Assault is about more than war. *Hannah Coulter* is about more than war. Those two books—and all the great books I was reading—were about the complexity and entirety of the human experience. About the things we wish to forget and those we want more and more of. About how we react and how we wish we could react. Books *are* experience, the words of authors proving the solace of love, the fulfillment of family, the torment of war, and the wisdom of memory. Joy and tears, pleasure and pain: everything came to me while I read in my purple chair. I had never sat so still, and yet experienced so much.

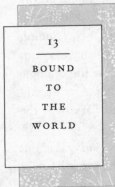

13

———

BOUND
TO
THE
WORLD

*I cried with joy when all the children began to
play together in the sparkling foam of the waves
that broke between worlds at the point. It was
beautiful, and that is a word I would not need to
explain to the girls from back home and I do not
need to explain to you, because now we are all
speaking the same language.*

CHRIS CLEAVE,
Little Bee

WHAT SERENDIPITY BROUGHT ME TO CHRIS CLEAVE'S
Little Bee halfway through my year of reading? I had begun my
year with *The Elegance of the Hedgehog*, and learned there my
first lesson, to find the beauty and to hold on to it for a lifetime.
And now I read *Little Bee*, where I learned that there is beauty
in the affinity of found connection between me and the rest of
the world. I, who often felt like an outsider, found myself to be
fully a part of the world and not apart from it.

Growing up in an immigrant household, I suppose it was
natural to feel like an alien in my midwestern town. But the
feeling persisted through college, law school, and even now as
a mother in another suburban town. My children weren't par-
ticularly sporty, and I wasn't one for joining clubs, and so I felt
left out of the flow of playdates, ball games, and cocktail parties that punctuated other families' lives. When my sister died,
the feeling of distance heightened. Everyone assured me that I
would feel better soon, that grieving was a process and I would
get through it. How did they know that? How could they know
that about *me*? I felt as if no one really understood what I was
going through.

But books were showing me that everyone suffers, at different times in their lives. And that yes, in fact, there were many people who knew exactly what I was going through. Now, through reading, I found that suffering and finding joy are universal experiences, and that those experiences are the connection between me and the rest of the world. My friends could have told me the same, I know, but with friends there are always barriers, hidden corners, and covered emotions. In books, the characters are made known to me, inside and out, and in knowing them, I know myself, and the real people who populate my world.

Little Bee tells the story of a young woman (Little Bee is her nickname) who has fled her home country of Nigeria and come to England to seek out Andrew and Sarah, the couple who saved her once before. But Andrew has committed suicide, and Sarah is suffering from depression. Not only has the death of Sarah's husband left her questioning the meaning of her own life, but her son persists in behaving bizarrely, her lover irritates her, and her job as a journalist seems pointless. Little Bee tries to offer commiseration and understanding, and in turn Sarah reaches out to offer support to Little Bee. Little Bee witnessed the rape and murder of her sister and the pillaging and destruction of her village, and is struggling to find a place, within and without, where she feels safe. Her past haunts her through memories, and her present—living undocumented and unemployed—is unstable.

Sarah and Little Bee both feel like outsiders. Sarah sees everyone around her as functioning on a different level, one she can't reach or understand. Little Bee is both literally an alien, as an undocumented refugee, and a foreigner to all the English people around her. She is further set apart by the horror she has had to experience.

In my first year as a lawyer in the late 1980s, I took on the case of an immigrant seeking refuge in the United States. Like Little Bee, Kulwinder Singh had a horrible story of torture to tell. Picked up by the police in the Punjab state of India, Kulwinder was suspected of being a member of a militant group seeking an independent Sikh state. He was held by the police for weeks and tortured repeatedly, then released with a warning. He scrounged together money for a plane ticket and, with his family's blessings, fled India. Upon arrival at JFK Airport in New York, he requested asylum and was placed in a detention center in downtown Manhattan. The first time I met him, I was struck by how little he was. The regulation orange overalls he'd been given were many sizes too large, and he'd rolled up the sleeves and legs in an attempt to find a fit. His face, unshaven and tired looking, was as small as a child's. We sat together with a translator, a turbaned Sikh who made clear his disdain for Kulwinder's short hair. The translator explained to me later, with a sniff, that true Sikhs never cut their hair.

Long hair or short, Kulwinder had suffered for his cultural identity. Through the stumbling words of his soft and tentative voice, I learned the details of his arrest and torture. During our allotted time together, spent in the dusty visitors' room of the detention center, I forced myself to study and document his scars. The back of his hands were marked with discolored and raised ridges of mottled skin, and on his palms I saw darkened circles where cigarettes had burned holes. The circular marks continued up along his arm, and when he pulled the legs of his overalls up, I could see more darkened dots on his thighs.

With the documentation of his scars and the words of his testimony, we won our case before the immigration judge. Kulwinder was granted asylum. He now lives quietly and safely in

New York State. The scars on his body are the closest to torture I have ever come, and I would never want to be any closer.

I don't believe that there is some grand karma, an invisible spirit or tether, that unites me with all other humans in the world. I know by experience that a horrible, devastating event can occur, and I will remain unaware of it. I didn't feel my sister's last breath passing across my cheek to let me know she was gone. I don't feel a rumble beneath my feet at the same time an earthquake strikes thousands of miles away or suffer sudden anguish when on the other side of the world genocide is being committed. I didn't feel Kulwinder being burned with cigarettes on the palms of his hands.

But even with all my ignorance, I know there are events in human experiences that I have been made to feel and to understand. It is done through the power of reading. How do books work their magic? How do writers bind their readers so tightly with their characters that we become those characters as we read? Even where—*especially* where—the characters and the plot are so different from our own lives?

By recognizing what is universal. Little Bee says to Sarah one morning as they drive from the house to buy milk, "We are all trying to be happy in this world. I am happy because I do not think the men will come to kill me today. You are happy because you can make your own choices." Little Bee and Sarah see themselves in the hopes of the other, and they want to help each other fulfill those hopes. I saw myself in both characters. I saw outsiders trying to find answers. It was not the physical or historical resemblances that mattered. It is our common desire, shared beneath the skin.

After the war, my father was a "displaced person," a refugee without passport or country. After living in a refugee camp, and then as a worker on an American army base, he moved in with a German couple. The couple had lost all of their children—three sons—in the war. They were very kind to my father, feeding him with whatever food could be scrounged to get meat back on his skinny frame and inviting him to sit with them in the evening as a member of the family. What my father shared with the husband and wife was a desire for peace and security. Together, the three of them tried to rebuild normalcy after the horrors of war.

Jack's father was stationed on an island in the Philippines after the war. He met Americans there who were charged with holding Japanese soldiers found guilty of war crimes and condemned to die. Somehow the American soldiers discovered that many of the Japanese prisoners were talented artists. The Americans showed the prisoners photos of their loved ones back in the States and asked the men to paint portraits from the photos. In exchange, the Americans gave the prisoners cigarettes and other luxuries to ease their last days. For the Americans, the exchange brought them closer to their families at home. For the Japanese, the exchange brought them recognition as talented and sharing human beings, not just animals caught up in the desecrations of war. The story reminds me of the line in *Hannah Coulter*, where even in the worst of the battle of Okinawa, there was "enormous pity that seemed to accumulate in the air."

Earlier in April I'd read *Ruins* by Achy Obejas, the story of an impoverished Cuban man in his fifties. Usnavy works every day at a bodega, filling the ration cards of the people who line up for goods: "Soap was scarce, coffee rare; no one could remember the last time there was meat." He lives in one room with his wife and daughter, a room without windows and where the floor is always damp from leaks. The communal bathroom of their tenement is enveloped in a constant swarm of flies, and the entire building is on the verge of collapse. Every day, Usnavy hears about more and more Cubans taking to the sea, escaping to America in search of better food, better housing, and a better future. Friends of Usnavy build themselves a flimsy raft, but he will not leave Cuba.

I could hardly imagine a person more unlike myself than Usnavy, and yet I identified with him. I sympathized with him and grieved with him. At the end, I found myself fervently hoping that his final wish could come true, to "die old and contented . . . in the soft dapple of a primal Antillean night." Obejas made me feel that Usnavy was a part of my own self because she found what we shared in common: love, hope, faith. He loves his family, and I love mine. He has hope for his future, as I do for my own. He has faith in Castro's revolution; I have faith in the power of books. The focus of our faith differs, but the support our faith gives to our lives does not.

The main character in Philip Roth's *Indignation*, Marcus, is another character with whom I have little in common. He is a Jewish boy from Newark experiencing college in the 1950s. And yet we are alike in how we love our parents, and hope for our futures. Marcus, like me, feels the weight of the trust that others hold in him. After Anne-Marie died, I wanted to reassure my parents and my kids that I would stay healthy. I wanted Jack to feel safe and secure in our marriage and for Natasha to call on me whenever and however she needed me. I willingly took on the responsibility of trying to assuage the pain and fear felt by those around me.

But Marcus begins to feel overwhelmed by the ambitions that his parents have for him and by what his friends want from him. Filial duty, religious dictates, conventions of society, the rules at his college, the sexual demands of his fellow students:

he cannot keep up with all that is expected of him, but he wants to, so much. In the end he rebels under the pressure, but his rebellion is his undoing. After he's followed the rules for so long, the one time he breaks all expectations brings the very worst outcome. He learns that sometimes our "most banal, incidental, even comical choices achieve the most disproportionate result." I cried with the truth of that statement—life is so unfair—and with its consequences for Marcus.

I finished *Indignation* sitting beside a yellow stretch of forsythia bushes in full bloom. The bushes line the back of our yard where there used to be a tangled mess of dead leaves and brambles, the property line marked by poison ivy, oriental bittersweet vines growing over misshapen pear trees, and weeds the size of bushes.

The first spring after we moved in, I spent weeks raking out the leaves and weeds and clearing the patch of its choking brambles and vines. I pruned back the pear trees and tossed the bottles, butts, and cans I'd found scattered among the overgrown vegetation into a trash bucket. I dug up boulders the size of football helmets and used them to block off a space for bushes and flowers. Into the holes left behind by the boulders I planted tiny sprigs of forsythia, bargain buys from my local nursery. I planted bleeding hearts and daffodils. My arms became covered with the itchy rash of poison ivy. My knees were gray with dirt no matter how hard I scrubbed, and my back muscles ached at night in bed.

As that spring warmed to summer, the forsythia turned green and grew fat and tall. The pear trees still bent at a funny angle, but their branches grew thick with leaves. Each spring since that year the daffodils and the bleeding hearts have come out again, every year more of them, and the pear trees have borne frothy white blossoms. The forsythia bushes burst out in yellow, brighter and bigger than the year before. I rarely prune back the wild branching. I love the way the yellow sprays reach out any which way for light and toss around in the wind. It is as if the bushes are dancing along the patch of lime green spring grass.

Reading my book a day this year was clearing my brain the way my hard work had cleared the mess in my backyard. I had been caught in a bramble patch of sorrow and fear. My reading, sometimes painful and often exhausting, was pulling me out of the shadows and into the light. And I am not the only one clearing out weeds and poison ivy, or planting beauty, perennial flowers of hope. The world is full of us, digging and scraping, working for the day when the flowers come back like they are supposed to, blooming year after year.

At the end of *Little Bee*, Sarah and Little Bee are on a beach in Nigeria. Little Bee falls asleep in the sun. She dreams: "I traveled through my country and I listened to stories of all kinds. Not all of them were sad. There were many beautiful stories that I found. There was horror, yes, but there was joy in them too. The dreams of my country are no different from yours—they are as big as the human heart."

Yes, Little Bee's heart was the same size as Sarah's. Just as my heart is the same size as the heart of Kulwinder Singh, and the heart of my father was the same size as the hearts of the couple in Regensburg who lost all their sons in the war. The hearts of the Japanese soldiers on the island in the Pacific were as big as the hearts of their captors. I am connected to the rest of humanity, not through a giant shared karma, but through our diverse experiences and yet communal emotions. By the size of our hearts.

Reading was making me see that my own loss and confusion were matched around the world by others struggling to make sense of the unexpected, the feared, and the unavoidable. How to live? With empathy. Because in sharing the load of that fear and confusion, isolation and sadness, I could lighten my own. Already the burden is lifting. My own desires are reseeding, my own needs rerooting. I am in a garden freed of brambles and weeds, and I am not alone. There are a bunch of us out there, weed-whacking away and ready for the sun.

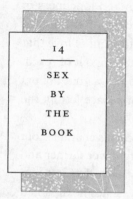

14

SEX
BY
THE
BOOK

After twelve years of marriage, Laura had become permanently tired of his enthusiasm. She'd realized if you gave an inch you were in for the mile, that even if you were occasionally available, he'd assume the welcome mat was always on the stoop.

JANE HAMILTON,
Laura Rider's Masterpiece

IF DESIRE WERE ONLY AN IMPULSE TO CONTINUE THE SPE-
cies, manifestations of it would have ceased once my children were born. The fact that desire survived the painful physical experience of having children underscores that our desire for sex is more than just a biological urge. With six people to shop and cook for, four children to watch over, a house to keep relatively clean, and a book a day to read and write about, I was short on time and drained of energy. Sex should not even have been part of my vocabulary, and yet it was. Where did the desire come from?

Early in my year of reading, I read *A Celibate Season* by Carol Shields and Blanche Howard. In the novel, a married couple with two teenage children spends ten months apart because of the wife's career. Jocelyn and Charles have the whole of Canada between them, and with finances tight (and e-mail still in the early stages), they decide to communicate only by letters. They have no doubts that they can maintain their loving connection via words alone.

But as the months of their separation pass, they find that the connection cannot be kept through letters alone. Even a phone call here and there is not enough. The pain and loneliness of separation combined with the desire for companionship lead both of them to bouts of adultery. It isn't falling out of love that has sent each into the arms of another; it is falling out of reach. Jocelyn has journeyed off without Charles, and nature abhors a vacuum. Another body must fill the empty space left by the vacant spouse.

Jim Harrison in *The English Major* also sets his character out on a journey alone. Cliff is a sixty-year-old former farmer and high school English teacher whose wife, Vivian, has left him for another man. Cliff decides to visit all the states he dreamed about as a child but has never seen. He starts out on his road trip with an ordered plan of a specific route to follow and things to do along the way. His plan is blown off course by the unexpected addition of Marybelle, an ex-student. Marybelle hitches a ride with Cliff and becomes not only a fellow passenger on his journey west but an instigator of wild sex and unanticipated layovers.

Cliff thinks a lot about sex. Why men want sex, why women do, and why desire flames up, fizzles out, and then starts up all over again. Cliff realizes that desire can be set off by something as simple as a smile. Sometimes the "worm" moves just because of a broad-backed waitress who beams ("not many women beam") or the memory of a babysitter's bikini-dressed bottom in his face one summer when she turned to get off the hot seat of his car: "Thirty years later her butt is still a vivid painting in my neurons."

I understood that. A remembered hand sliding across my thigh under the table of a college pub is enough to start the shivers down my spine. It is the power of memory—tactile memories of desire stirred—that gives potency to the descriptions of seduction I read in books. Even where there is no recorded memory, new sensations of desire can be felt through words alone. There was a time a few years ago when I thought about putting up a Web site of "get in the mood" stories for all the women I met who told me that their initially fervent ardor for their mates was fading away.

"I love him," one friend told me, "but I no longer want him."

I nixed the idea of writing to stir the loins of others because there were already authors who wrote so well about sex. Instead, I told my friends to have a glass of wine, read a juicy story of lovemaking from a good book, and then grab their beloved.

"Read *The Sailor from Gibraltar* by Marguerite Duras or *The Delta of Venus* by Anaïs Nin," I suggested. "Or *How Stella Got Her Groove Back* by Terry McMillan." Stella has to journey to Jamaica and find a young stud to find ardor again, but for those without a travel budget, books alone can bring the groove back on. Just in the past month I'd read *Waiting in Vain* by Colin Channer. There was plenty of great—and innovative—birds-and-bees action in that book. Enough to inspire blazing renewals of physical devotion in even the most dated of relationships.

Such a book might have come in handy for Laura Rider, the main character in Jane Hamilton's *Laura Rider's Masterpiece*. For Laura, desire in a marriage has a shelf life. When the date is past, desire expires, gone for good. She loves her husband, but "just as a horse has a finite number of jumps in her, so Laura had used up her quota." Laura takes "the welcome mat" off the stoop and lets her husband know sex is no longer an option between them. The only problem with Laura's declaration of her spent desire is that her husband is not finished yet. He still wants sex, he wants it to be part of love, and he falls in love—and into bed—with another woman. Their lives fall into chaos, and people get hurt.

Cliff in *The English Major* never tires of sex, but he does come to understand that "given more than enough sex you see that it isn't the be all and end all of human existence." Sex is just one of the bindings that holds a marriage together, but it is a pretty good one. Cliff and his wife come back to each other by the end of the novel, reeled in by the history they share, by their ease and comfort with each other, and by their festering mutual desire. As Cliff explains it, love, friendship, and an accumulation of years spent together count for a lot. But sex counts for something too.

I never talked about sex with my parents or with my sisters, not as a teenager and not later, as a woman. When I was in high school, I listened as my friends offered hints and bits of information, but nothing they said seemed quite right to me. I found out what I needed to know from books. I read the hot and sweaty stuff, all heaving breasts, taut nipples, and long members, but often the writing was so bad I doubted I could trust the images. I read *Fear of Flying* by Erica Jong and laughed throughout, but I was not interested in having zipless, mindless sex.

I went on a Graham Greene binge in high school, reading *A Burnt-Out Case*, *The Heart of the Matter*, *The End of the Affair*, and *The Power and the Glory*. When accompanied by love, sex in Greene's world is a gift from God, but it is always second to a greater love, love for God. Sex without love is a perversion of its purpose (to make life). Okay, sex with love, I understood the equation and I liked it. But when I went off to college I didn't quite apply the equation correctly. When the sex happened first, I faked the love to salve my guilt over having loveless sex.

Faked love brought melodrama into my life, marked by mood swings, drinking binges, and ugly scenes of very bad breakups.

The book that saved me in college, many times and over and over, was *Burger's Daughter* by Nadine Gordimer. The novel offers so much to emulate in the title character, Rosa Burger. Rosa is struggling to define herself and her future after the death of her father, a prominent antiapartheid activist. She is fleeing both the celebrity and the weight of inherited duty brought on by being the daughter of a famous and influential man. Rosa is tempted to remove herself from the socially responsible and politically committed life she grew up in and to carve out a quiet, uneventful existence for herself.

At one point in the novel, Rosa travels to the south of France to visit her father's first wife. There she begins an affair. She falls in love. But it is more the ease of the relationship, its privacy and its anonymity, that seduces her into love, rather than the man himself. There is nothing lofty or inspired in their love, only normalcy and peace. Rosa finds solace in being part of a couple among countless couples: "In the heat they had shut out, people were eating in soft clatter, laughter, and odours of foods that had been cooked in the same way for so long their smell was the breath of the stone houses. Behind other shutters other people were also making love."

Rosa considers settling in the south of France and leaving South Africa forever behind in her past: "It's possible to live within the ambit of a person not a country." But her past will not let her rest in a retired existence of satiety and comfort. She feels a connection to South Africa, and she returns to the country of her youth to fulfill the commitment made long ago by her father.

Rosa became a guiding character for me, and informed many of my thoughts about my own life goals and dreams. Her understanding of love and sex as a place of quiet comfort and hidden joy resonated deeply, providing a jarring example to my own explosive and painful affairs. I slowed down, let love come to me, and, more or less (there was a learning curve), contained my desire within relationships of kindness and affection. I wasn't always a loyal girlfriend, but when I cheated, it wasn't because desire overcame my good sense. It was because love had faded and I was too much of a chicken to break off the relationship.

I first kissed Jack on New Year's Eve 1988. He'd been a good friend for months, both of us logging long hours at the law firm where we worked. The two of us were at the office on the last day of the year, and I'd invited him to come out with me to a big party in a mansion overlooking the Hudson. It was a black-tie party. For a joke, I gave Jack a blue-and-red polka-dot bow tie to wear. At midnight he loosened the ridiculous bow and then grabbed me with both arms, drawing me in close for a long kiss. On the ride back to Manhattan he tried to work his way down the row of sixty buttons on my black velvet dress but had made it through only ten buttons—just below my clavicle—when the cab reached his apartment. One month later we were in Utah together, holed up in the honeymoon suite at the Snowed Inn. It was the only room available, and we took it as a benediction of our desire. Sex with love: the perfect equation.

Maybe one day I'll find myself wondering what someone else would be like. It is human nature, after all, to be drawn to an opposite of what you have in hand. As Antonya Nelson notes in her story "Palisades," from the collection *Female Trouble*, "You wanted to be sitting in a comfortable leather recliner sipping fine wine and reading a passage of exquisite prose to your wise spouse for your mutual amusement, and you wanted to be having demeaning speed-demon sex in a seedy dorm room with a gorgeous soulless youth. . . . You wanted something solid; you wanted something fluid." But wondering is not wandering, and my desire is not waning. What holds a couple together is more than just ardor—it is the confabulation of two, a conversation spanning years, sometimes carried out through words and sometimes through caresses.

In the end, it is the acknowledgment of their years of mutual experiences—as parents, as friends, as husband and wife— that bring Cliff and Vivian back together in *The English Major*. They are each happy in their own space with their own interests, but acknowledge their ties of desire and a mutual history. Jocelyn and Charles from *A Celibate Season* also make it through their crises more or less intact. They come together again physically and mentally, bound by "all the little threads of concern and necessity" of their shared past. They never lost their ardor for each other. It's more as if it were misplaced, and then found again.

Where does desire come from? In the books I was reading, it came from many points of stimulus, both physical and mental. Words stirred ardor, as surely as a hand across a breast. But how to hold on to desire?

Desire comes from love between two people, and also gives back to the bonds between them. Ardor waxes and wanes, and I could understand Laura Hamilton feeling as if her quota has been met. There are times when I'd rather read a book than jump into bed, and I'd certainly rather read a book a day than have sex every single day for a year. But I also know—and the books I was reading proved me right—that sex strengthens the connections between my husband and me, adding muscle and flexibility and longevity to a union that is based on much more than just a physical need.

Jack and I are together because we love each other and what we have made out of our love is a place within the world where we are safe—or as safe as we can be. After losing Anne-Marie, I know the limits of security, but I want to be held as tightly as possible within those limits of love and caring. Welcome mat outside the door, a flag against danger and a beacon for life.

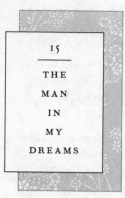

15

THE
MAN
IN
MY
DREAMS

*Here is the old argument . . . "Death is sweet,
it delivers us from the fear of death." Is this not
a comfort? No, it is a sophistry. Or rather, proof
that it will take more than logic, and rational
argument, to defeat death and its terrors.*

JULIAN BARNES,
Nothing to Be Frightened Of

IN LATE MAY, THE NORTHERN ALLEY OF TREES IN THE CON-
servatory Garden in New York City's Central Park is shad-
owed by twisting black branches heavy with green leaves. The
stone-paved path between benches is littered with fallen apple
blossoms, past bloom, and the bordering ivy is thick, rising up
the tree trunks like clinging hands desperate for rescue. Under
the third tree on the right, the bench dedicated to Anne-Marie
waits, inscribed with her name and with the words she spoke
to Marvin when together they strolled this alley between trees:
"For who can end in despair when there is such beauty in the
world?"

My family meets every year on the anniversary of her death
at this bench in the park. This year the date fell on a Tuesday. It
was a nice day, warm and sunny. On the train into New York,
I read short stories of George Saunders collected in *Pastoralia*.
Saunders's characters are tortured by how life has not quite
panned out for them. They are the unfairly unloved, the hesitant bystanders, or the family caretakers no one cares about.
But Saunders's characters hang in there, certain that eventually life will swing their way. They feel an unwarranted—and

admirable—optimism. One of the characters in "Sea Oak" dies before getting the just rewards she was so sure of. And so she comes back from the dead as a decomposing corpse to claim what is hers. She is mad as hell, and she isn't going to take it anymore: "Some people get everything and I got nothing. Why? Why did that happen?" She may be dead, but she is still kicking. Fiction or possibility?

I have always hoped for the possibility of some sort of existence after death. When I read the title of Julian Barnes's memoir of his own struggle with mortality, *Nothing to Be Frightened Of*, it made sense to me as a genuine statement of fear. Since childhood, it has been the *nothingness* that comes after death that frightens me. When I was twelve, I had a dream so vivid that I still remember every detail. I'm at home, standing in the raised doorway between our dimly lit one-car garage and the book-lined study. A man stands next to the shelves in front of my father's chess table. He stands where the wooden-framed dome-shaped chair with the green cushion belongs but that now has somehow disappeared. He is glaring at me with angry eyes, and his mouth is a thin line of hate. He moves toward me. Holding a gun to my head with one hand, he restrains me with the other, preventing me from running away. I feel the gun against the side of my head, and I know then what death will be. A darkness, an eternal void, an ending of all thought. Behind the man are all the books I will never read; in front of me, blankness forever.

Barnes deals with his own fear of nothingness by becoming a troubled agnostic: "I don't believe in God, but I miss him." He wonders if his transformation from atheist to maybe-believer is a function of age (the closer death comes, the better an afterlife looks) or of intellect. He can't find proof of life after death, but neither can he find disproving evidence.

I love Barnes's story about an atheist getting to the gates of heaven after dying and being pretty pissed off about it all: "Watch the Fury of the Resurrected Atheist." I wouldn't be angry at all to find pearly gates and endless clouds and the faces of friends and family who'd passed over years before. I know I'd be deliriously relieved and giddy with excitement. I can buy the argument that there are many dimensions we cannot fathom, and that the spirits of those who have died can hover about in those dimensions, appearing as a remembrance or in that déjà vu feeling we are all familiar with. I know my sister comes to me in dreams. I just wish she would come as a perfectly viewed apparition. I wouldn't scream, I promise. I would grab her, wispy bits of air or not, and hold on.

Natasha met me by the clock at the center of Grand Central.

"Do you ever feel as if Anne-Marie is still hovering?" I asked her.

"Yes, of course," she answered quickly, and then was silent for a moment before continuing. "I know she's here when we talk about her."

We walked up to the Conservatory Garden in Central Park, entering through the wrought-iron gate at 105th Street. We turned right and entered the northern alley of apple trees, almost past their time of flowering, and found our parents already there, sitting on Anne-Marie's bench.

Red roses had been tied onto the bench, and we added our own white roses and a thick bunch of rosemary held by an electric blue ribbon. Rosemary for remembrance.

"Do you remember when we all came here just after Peter turned one?"

"Peter in his little plaid pants and jacket. He ran all over the garden, and Anne-Marie followed him everywhere."

There is a picture of us from that day, the three sisters. We are sitting on a bench like this one, but in the southern alley of trees. In the photo we are glowing, smiling, holding confidently onto each other as if we had all the time in the world to talk, laugh, and hold on. Now I ask someone passing by to take a photo. He nods, smiling, and snaps the picture. Two sisters remaining, a mother, a father. Red and white roses, deep green branch of rosemary, a slash of blue ribbon: the colors frame us against the black of the bench.

Was Anne-Marie there with us? Could she be? In the year after Anne-Marie died, I came to this bench in the fall to sit by myself. I looked up to see a raccoon overhead, peaceful and secure, clinging comfortably to the branch above me. That raccoon was either very real or it was an apparition of Anne-Marie, her spirit counseling me. When I came again to the bench a few months later, this time with a friend, I sat down and cried. Suddenly a hard branch came flying out of nowhere and hit me on the head. I looked at my friend.

"Did you see that? Anne-Marie hit me! She's telling me to stop crying."

My friend nodded, her eyes opened wide. I stopped crying.

I looked up now, on this fourth anniversary, to see the green leaves filtering out the sun and the last blossoms of faded pink against the blue sky. New life after a long winter. Another message for me. Sent by a spirit or by nature?

Ghost or not, Anne-Marie still occupies a space in my life. In *Grief* by Andrew Holleran, the narrator describes grief as being "like Osiris; cut up in parts and thrown into the Nile. It fertilizes in ways we cannot know, the pieces of flesh bleed into every part of our lives, flooding the earth, till eventually Life appears once more." Osiris, god of the afterlife, offering a rebirth. I think of memories as working that way, of bringing Anne-Marie back before me. No, she is not reborn. And she is probably not a ghost drifting above me, or an angel singing in heaven. But nor is she *nothing*, and there is not *nothing* after her death. There are all my recollected moments of time I spent with her.

Jack and I spent a lot of our weekends out in Bellport with Anne-Marie and Marvin before we had kids. Bellport is a quiet town on the eastern end of Long Island, facing out across the Great South Bay to the dunes of Fire Island. From Anne-Marie's house, we could hear boat lines jangling in the wind off the bay, and the smell of salty marshes wafted through the house at night on breezes.

During the summer we went sailing on Marvin's sailboat or took the town ferry over to Fire Island to play in the ocean. We'd stay on the beach until the last ferry home and then stay up late at night, preparing and eating meals of crab legs, clams, pasta, and tomatoes picked that morning by kids working the local farm stands. After dinner we'd move out to the screened porch with bottles of wine, beer, and scotch, and talk until early in the morning.

When we visited in the winter, days were spent indoors by a fire, all of us reading books and drinking hot tea, or tramping through the small towns that surrounded Bellport, scouting out tag sales and book sales. One weekend I bought the complete set of *Personality Development: A Practical Self-Teaching Course*, published in the 1930s. The slim volumes were full of surprisingly wide-ranging advice, like how to pop a blackhead ("Cover the tips of the fingers with clean gauze or linen and press gently to expel the offending material") and how to choose a book to read ("Be serious, earnest, sincere in your choice of books, and then put your trust in Providence and read with an easy mind"). When I read out loud the section on how to pick up a fallen item with decorum ("Don't clutch or grab the article but pick it up lightly and gracefully with the fingertips"), Anne-Marie burst out laughing and right away threw a napkin to the floor, allowing me an opportunity to practice.

I remembered showing up at Anne-Marie's door the day Gorbachev was overthrown in a coup and Hurricane Bob came hurtling up the Eastern Seaboard. Jack and I were running away from our rented hut on the farthest reaches of Long Island and arrived in Bellport looking for refuge. All was quiet, with no sign of Anne-Marie or Marvin. We called and called for them, and finally I headed upstairs to look.

Anne-Marie emerged from her bathroom, dripping wet from the shower.

"A coup? A hurricane? What are you talking about?" Within minutes the power went out, and after waking Marvin, we all went down to huddle in the kitchen.

The only food in the house was oysters pulled just yesterday from the sea, salty crackers, and day-old bread. There was no milk and no way to make coffee without power.

"At least we have plenty of champagne," Anne-Marie offered. So we survived on oysters and champagne and some smelly cheese Anne-Marie dug out of the back of the fridge. We lit candles, made a fire, and had a wonderful day while the wind howled outside. By the next morning electricity cranked through the house, Gorbachev was on his way back to power, and the sun was shining.

When we started having kids, Jack and I were still invited out to Bellport, despite all the equipment we dragged with us (travel crib, high chair, stroller, bags and bags of diapers, clothes, toys), to say nothing of our loud and boisterous little beasts. The adults still stayed up late drinking and talking out on the porch, but the mornings came much earlier than anyone wanted, especially when punctuated by the noises of little children eager for movement and talk and play. I'd try to hustle the kids out of the house, shushing them all the way, taking them to the world's coldest diner for breakfast (we took our winter fleeces along to keep warm) and then driving over to the beachside playground. We stayed there until a decent hour had been reached and we could return home to our second breakfast, the blueberry pancakes that Anne-Marie always made for the boys when we visited.

Anne-Marie used to sit down on the floor with the boys, one at a time. Taking one foot in each of her hands, she would make the feet talk to each other. The feet spoke in little whiny voices, complaining of injustice ("Why do I always have to wear the sock with the hole?") and arguing back and forth ("You smell!" "No, you smell worse!"). The kids laughed so hard and stuck out their feet, asking for more. And more she would give them, tirelessly.

In remembering Anne-Marie, I hold a warrant against the worst death has to offer. I laugh when remembering the funny stuff, smile at the thought of all her kindnesses, and I find courage for tomorrow, and for the hereafter. There is no void where there is memory. After I die, someone will remember me and bring me back. Maybe I will be a spirit, floating around in the ether around my kids, goading them on to remember me (*she read a book a day for a whole year—what a nut!*), but maybe not. And if there is a gunman out there, waiting to cut off my life and keep me away from the books on the shelves, for now I am safe. I have pulled the purple chair in front of him, backed up against his glaring eyes. I am sitting down and reading my fill of books. And remembering. And keeping myself, and the person who was Anne-Marie, alive. I have nothing to be frightened of.

Like today, she remembers, it was so quiet at
home, just the two of them with the whole day to
themselves, and she was so sure of what she had to
do: teach him everything, make him laugh, make
him feel that he was safe and watched over.

RON SUSKIND,
A Hope in the Unseen

EARLY IN JUNE, GEORGE HAD A BAND PERFORMANCE. HE'D
been playing the tuba for months, and I liked the sound of it.
His instructor assured me that playing the unwieldy instrument was a sure "in" to college: "Tuba players are rare and necessary," he told me. I wasn't thinking about George getting into college yet, and I already knew he was rare and necessary. But I really did like the resonating reach of the deep *boom*s and *bahm*s that came from George's tuba.

The concert kicked off a stream of end-of-school-year events. Exams and a prom for Peter; graduations for George and Michael, elementary school and middle school; a beach party for Martin. My kids were growing up. I'd have them home with me this summer, but our days of entwined hours spent together were dwindling. My boys' lives were spreading out, away from me, and into places where I couldn't go. Places I wasn't invited. Places I couldn't protect them.

There is a terrifying scene in one of Greg Bottoms's short stories in *Fight Scenes*, which I read in early June, where a young boy defaces a photo of himself and leaves it on his mother's refrigerator. His friend observes that "if a mother had any idea of what her son's life was like, what his thoughts were like, what he was like, he might kill her by breaking her heart." I hoped that none of my children had lives or thoughts that would break my heart. I wanted fresh air and happiness for them, and no dark nights or choked thinking. Whatever protection I could offer now came in the values that I'd tried to instill, through sharing and teaching and example. But what had I instilled?

I have a drawing hanging up in my bedroom that Peter made for me the first summer we lived in Westport. The drawing is titled "Mom Making Dinner," and it shows me with baby Martin in one arm. He is bawling his head off, with large oval teardrops falling off into space. With my other arm I am reaching helplessly for a salad bowl that is cascading to the floor, all the salad leaves floating around it in a halo of greens. My mouth is wide open in full Edvard Munch *Scream* mode, and my eyes look a bit wild. But despite the O-shaped mouth and rabies-reminiscent eyes, I look happy. I'm light on my feet, dancing barefoot across the blank white of the page.

My life for so long was that drawing, mishaps and mayhem and screams but also laughter, togetherness, and light. Lots of light.

The light still shone for me whenever I looked at my kids, but our moments of building Lego towns and making up new cake recipes (each more sickening than the last) and reading out loud before bed were over. Okay, so we still made Jell-O chocolate pudding as a team: one to stir, one to pour, one to bring to the fridge, one to ladle on the whipped cream before serving, and one to clean up (me). And we still all had dinner together, although it was chicken paillard now instead of nuggets, and my mixed salad managed to make it to the table intact in its bowl.

All the easy talk that used to happen over dinner had been replaced by the boys telling me what they wanted to tell me, when they wanted to. Of course I had never been fully privy to what their thoughts were, but when they were little, they'd prattle on and on about whatever was on their minds. Now I had to rely on whatever words they'd parse out over meals, or resort to more modern forms of expression, like texting and Facebook. Peter allowed me to be his friend on Facebook, but with the threat that if he felt as if I were stalking him, he'd de-friend me.

"Don't stalk me, either!" I'd replied.

"Yeah, right, Mom. Like I'm going to spend my time reading your profile page."

No, I knew he wasn't going to waste his time spying on me. But what was he going to waste his time on? I knew so much about my children, but what terrified me was what I didn't know. What good examples or advice had I passed on to them? I wondered what had stuck with them, of all the life lessons I'd lobbed their way.

I know my kids love to read, like I do. When we still lived in New York City, every morning Jack and I walked the boys to PS 9 on the Upper West Side. Then Jack would continue on to the office, and I would head home with George, not yet old enough to go to school. One morning as we were walking, Peter was reading a book and trying to keep up with us at the same time.

"Peter," Jack admonished, "you can't read and walk at the same time."

Peter nodded, and we continued on. I noticed after a few minutes that Peter wasn't with us. I turned around to see him at the end of the block, head in his book. Given the choice of reading or walking—he couldn't do both—he'd chosen to read.

I saw in the books I was reading this year both what I hoped for my children, and what I feared for them. In a swirling of voices and scenes, I found guidance not only for my life but for what I wanted in theirs. In *The Picts and the Martyrs* by Arthur Ransome, I read about a perfect summer spent outdoors, freed from supervision and rules. Ransome wrote twelve Swallows and Amazons books between 1929 and 1947, about the kids from two families, the "Swallows" from the Walker family and the "Amazons" referring to the two Blackett girls. All my English friends read these books when they were kids, and sometimes I think the childhood memories they shared with me were actually taken straight from Ransome's novels. And why not? The kids in Ransome's books have great times together.

Defiant of adult intervention, Ransome's characters set their own course for fun. "We're free to start stirring things up. We'll hoist the skull and crossbones again the moment we've had our grub. We'll get things moving without wasting a minute." The kids take care of themselves and of each other, having a good time and getting along with very little bickering or whining. Ransome is known for his practical details, and this novel included specifics on how to sail, how to catch trout with your hands, and how to skin a rabbit (not easily). The kids in *The Picts and the Martyrs* behave as I hope my own kids would, with bravery and common sense and joy.

In Junot Díaz's *Brief Wondrous Life of Oscar Wao*, which I read a few days later, a much darker portrait of an independent childhood is presented. Oscar is a teenager hounded by his mother but then left much on his own to defend and define himself on the streets of Newark. The kids in Ransome's books always have the safety net of their family (or the family cook), but Oscar is on his own. His father disappeared years ago, and his mother relates to both Oscar and his sister only through threats and anger: "It was her duty to keep me crushed under her heel." The sole loving person in Oscar's life is his grandmother, and she lives across the sea in the Dominican Republic. To his grandmother, he is a "genius"; to everyone else, he is a mutant: "You really want to know what being an X-man feels like? Just be a smart bookish boy of color in a contemporary U.S. ghetto. Mamma mia! Like having bat wings or a pair of tentacles growing out of your chest."

My book group in Westport read *A Hope in the Unseen* by Ron Suskind for our June meeting. *A Hope in the Unseen* is a nonfiction account of a boy raised by a single mother in one of the worst neighborhoods in Washington, D.C. Cedric, like Oscar, is something of a mutant, jeered at by the kids at school for his good grades, held up like a specimen of good behavior by his teachers, and misunderstood by his incarcerated father. His mother is his main support, and she is generous with her love and affection. Food and shelter, however, are harder to supply. Some nights there is no dinner because there is no money for food. The pair face eviction and homelessness more than once.

Although there are similarities between Oscar and Cedric, Cedric has the unfailing support, if not always understanding, of his mother. Cedric's moment of becoming a man is, for me, when he understands that whatever he wants to leave behind in his past, his mother is "not something to rise above and leave behind. She's what got him this far. Give, give, give her whole life, mostly to him." He says to her now, "You can't be the only one doing the caring. I'm strong enough to do some now, too." Then he hugs her: "His long arms squeeze tight around her, a big woman who doesn't need to be so damn big anymore."

From a place of hope and love grows a man. Cedric was

cared for, and in turn becomes a man who can take care of himself, and of others. An example set by a mother and replicated by a son. What examples am I setting? A book a day for a year: obsessive and crazy, or dedicated and disciplined? It was up to my kids to decide for themselves.

One very rainy day in the fall, back before I'd started my book-a-day project, I went out to the side of the road by our house and started to dig away at the roots of a maple tree growing up in the shade of bigger trees. It was a tiny tree, but with beautiful red and orange leaves that glistened spectacularly in the rain. I worked away at the root ball of that tree and finally dug the whole thing out. I dragged the tree and the huge chunk of dirt hanging onto its roots into a wagon and then pulled the wagon across the lawn and out to the back of our house. I planted the tree beside the patio. From the kitchen sink, I could look out and see the brilliant leaves against the dark blue autumn sky. In winter, the branches caught snow that glittered under the sun. In springtime, tiny thin buds came out on its branches, and now, in June, the skinny tree was abundantly green. It provided just enough shade in one corner of the patio for me to pull a chair into and read, out of the sun. My kids had asked about that tree: Why hadn't I just gone to the nursery and bought a nice tree?

"Because," I explained to them, "this little maple was growing out under the shade by our big maples. It wasn't going to get any bigger out there, but it could get bigger. With more sun and air and space it could grow tall. So there it was, a tree with potential, and I saved it. That tree cost only the effort of my digging it up, lugging it over here, and planting it in the ground. Do you understand?"

"You don't have money for a new tree?" asked Martin.

"You're cheap?" tried George.

"You love to dig," Michael said in conclusion. Peter just shook his head. Jack came outside and offered another explanation.

"Your mother is crazy."

"All of the above," I said, "and I wanted shade on the patio."

I read Francine du Plessix Gray's biography *Madame de Staël: The First Modern Woman* under the shade of that tree. Just like me, and like most mothers, the mother of Madame de Staël was hell-bent on raising her child the right way. In figuring out how to raise my kids, I relied on the example of my own mother and of the mothers I liked in books, like the character of Geraldine Colshares in Laurie Colwin's *Goodbye Without Leaving*.

I felt a kinship to Geraldine. She'd been a backup singer and dancer for a rhythm and blues duo, and I'd always dreamed of being one. Once she gets married and has a kid, she wants only to hang out with her baby, Little Franklin: "Asleep on my arms, he was unaware that the person holding him was out of a job, had no profession, and had in fact outlived an era. Little Franklin of course didn't care, and I didn't much care either. I had a purpose in life: to sit in a rocking chair mindlessly musing on my baby while I nursed him and burped him and rocked him."

Yes, that was exactly how I felt when the boys were little. So maybe I wasn't looking to books for guidance on how to be a mother, as much as for approval on how I was doing it. Either way, reading Gerry's take on how motherhood was just like being in a band—"being very tired and singing a lot. Also being on your feet all the time"—made me feel better about being the mom that I was, and I sang louder than ever.

The mother of Madame de Staël also relied on books to figure out how to raise her daughter. She turned to the writing of Jean-Jacques Rousseau, and especially the guidelines he set forth in his novel *Émile*, to steer her child straight toward a fulfilling existence. According to biographer Gray, the mother misinterpreted Rousseau's dictates completely, but never mind. Her daughter came out of childhood with high wit, fast intelligence, big ambitions, and most of all, great enthusiasms.

Madame de Staël wrote in a letter, "Enthusiasm is the emotion that offers us the greatest happiness, the only one that offers it to us." I've tried to instill in my own kids unguarded glee about and curiosity in what happens around them every day. After all, what is curiosity but an enthusiasm to learn and to know?

Anne-Marie had boundless energy and endless curiosity for new ideas and new ways of looking at things. That enthusiasm drove her in her work, and in her relationships, although its flip side—her boredom with old tropes on tired themes—sometimes made spending time with her unnerving. I'd sat through dinners where she got up from the table, fed up with stagnant conversation and in search of someone more stimulating to talk to. For those of us who knew her well, the signal was clear: change the topic or else. It wasn't hard to find a new topic. Anne-Marie was always ready—and enthusiastic—for new ideas, and happy to come back to the table. I want my kids to be more diplomatic at dinner parties, but to be always open, like their aunt and like Madame de Staël, to new and different ideas and visions and goals.

I also want my children to feel grateful for all that life offers. In *The Laws of Evening* by Mary Yukari Waters, I found beautiful illustrations of such gratitude. The stories in *The Laws of Evening* are set mostly in Japan, ranging in period from the days before World War II through the war to the years after. Waters's characters have witnessed death on scales ranging from intimate (children, father, mother, spouse) to national (the horror of Hiroshima). None of her characters is fearful of death, but they display different responses of expectations, regret, or acceptance: "And she was thankful to whoever had left this signpost to testify that he, too, had known this limbo for which there are no words; that through the ages others had known it and that by her own humble path, she had come to the right place."

Despite their varied interpretations of death, Waters's characters share a reverence for life. They are deeply grateful to be alive. As one character explains, "The dappled leaf shadows moving over the earth like dark cells, the entirety of this garden harmonizing and fusing . . . In the end, being alive is what matters."

One of Waters's characters quotes a haiku by Mizuta Masahide, a seventeenth-century samurai and renowned writer of haikus. I seriously considered having the verse painted over our kitchen doorway: "Since my house burned down / I now own a better view / of the rising moon." A better view: that is what I wanted my kids to have. Not to see the worst of what circumstances rendered for them in their lives, but the best. Resilience in the face of disappointment.

What else did I want for my children? Haruki Murakami writes in his memoir *What I Talk About When I Talk About Running* about how, having decided to become a writer, he stuck to his goal with singularity: "You really need to prioritize in life, figuring out in what order you should divide up your time and energy. If you don't get that sort of system set by a certain age, you'll lack focus and your life will be out of balance." Having decided that for him writing would be the focus of life, he dedicated himself to it, understanding that there would be other aspects of life that he must give up. He can't give up running (prone to chubbiness, he runs to keep the weight off), but so-cializing and staying up late at night are activities he cuts out of his routine.

"He doesn't try to do it all," I explained to Jack that evening at dinner.

We'd had a special meal in honor of George's birthday, a continuation of days of festivities in his honor. There had been a party at school, a get-together that afternoon for friends, and now this dinner with his family. Over the weekend there would be one more celebration with my parents and Natasha. I'd made a slew of ice-cream cakes and invested in an allot-ment of Nerf guns and ammo (bubbles and piñatas wouldn't do it this year). I'd hung the birthday banner that would now decorate our kitchen through the summer. All four boys were born in the summer months, and Jack's birthday at the end of August rounded out the season. The weekend—and the sum-mer—was just starting, and I was already exhausted.

Do it all? Who was I kidding? Between Meredith, the four boys, and my parents, most weekends our house is filled to bursting. In the summer more guests come, mattresses laid out across floors and towels piled high in bathrooms. Food is in constant demand, with milk, bananas, orange juice, and bread at the top of the list every single day. Mess builds up, spread-ing throughout all the rooms: spread-eagled books and dis-membered toys, used glasses and discarded newspapers, and laundry, laundry everywhere. Kids track in dirt and leaves, and cats throw up in corners, leaving chewed-up grass in tiny mounds of offering. Every two weeks a Brazilian friend comes to the house, setting her cleaning crew to work with an effi-ciency and discipline I envy. Within twenty-four hours after they leave, chips have been retrod into the rug, cooking oil has splattered its way over the oven and across the counters, and another cat has thrown up another hard day's work of chewing.

"No one wants you to try and do it all," Jack said to me firmly, watching as I licked the last of the ice-cream cake from the tin tray. I had better start running, I thought to myself, adding one more daily activity to the list.

"You mean I shouldn't try to read and write and see friends and hang out with the kids and feed the family and do the laundry and cook great meals—"

Snorts from Peter and Michael, but I forged on.

"And keep the house from absolute neglect and filth, weed the garden, and make the beds—"

"Hey," interrupted Martin. "I make my bed, and I help with weeds."

"Yeah," said George, "and I made the treat bags for my birthday party. I always make my bed, *and* I bring my dirty clothes to the laundry room."

"You all have been great," Jack said. "I know Mom appreciates all your help." A look over to me.

"Yeah, I do," I said.

And I realized George was right. He had put the treat bags together all by himself, and come up with all the activities for his party. I'd only had to supply the artillery. Jack would cook lunch for our weekend party, and the older boys were on cleanup duty. No one had complained or probably even noticed that the birthday banner this year was not adorned with the multicolored streamers or pumped-up balloons I'd always added on in years past.

A year ago the clutter of postcards, coupons, and school flyers moldering away on my kitchen counter, the piles of school papers and projects and bills growing higher on my dining room table, and the dancing gray elephants of dust in the corner (to say nothing of the regurgitated grass) would have driven me mad. But this year, I sighed dramatically and said, "What the hell—I've got better things to do."

Somehow, in some miracle wrought by reading, my messier life was affording me a better view of the rising moon. It was a very, very good trade.

"I'm lucky. I'm doing what I love, reading a book every day. And you guys are helping me do that. I bet Murakami never gets the kind of help I get. That's what a family does—helps each other."

"Are you lecturing us?" George asked, his eyebrows shooting sky high and his mouth making a straight line of consternation.

"No, I'm thanking you." Okay, maybe I was lecturing. But I was also sharing. Sharing everything I was learning during this year of reading books, every chance I got. We were figuring things out together, making it work. Resilience, enthusiasm, gratitude, focus, independence. A strong foundation of family love. I'd found these components repeated, again and again, in the books I was reading. The ingredients for a satisfying life. And I'd added a little household mess into the mix, a leavening agent for the filling cake of existence.

On the last day of June I read Ernest Hemingway's *Nick Adams Stories*. In the story titled "On Writing," I found an homage to summer as it should be, and I remembered my own Midwest summers. Mornings spent out on the grass of our backyard, reading in ratty old lawn chairs; afternoons spent down at the beach, swimming in the cold waters of Lake Michigan; evenings when we hung out on the back patio, feeling the heat of a midsummer night settle in around us, playing Monopoly and Life, talking and laughing until late.

I wanted that again, summer days spent "just lying around,"

like Nick Adams. I still had my kids home with me, for at least one more summer. There would be more birthdays to celebrate and cakes to bake, more places I had to drive, more meals I had to cook, and more clothes I had to launder. But I would make sure to also make time for all of us to go swimming or play a game or just lie around in the hammock or on the grass, reading. Our times spent together would never be forgotten, and the lessons of love and security, of easy bliss and simple joys, would always be remembered.

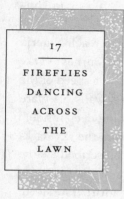

Maou cannot help but think of nighttime as it was
then, there in Onitsha: the fear and jubilation it
gave her, a shiver along her skin. Every night,
since their return to the south, it is the same shiver
which reunites her with what has been lost.

J. M. G. LE CLÉZIO,
Onitsha

LIVING IN A BEACH COMMUNITY, MY FAMILY DOESN'T USU-
ally go away in the summer. But during this summer of reading a book a day, I was getting myself away, far away. Books
were my comfort this year, and my counselors in how to live,
but they were also providing the vacations that I needed. In
the hours while the kids were at camp, hanging out in their
rooms, or running wild through the yard, I was traveling
across miles and across years, and finding new and old places
to visit. "There is no frigate like a book, / To take us lands
away," wrote Emily Dickinson. I was taking that frigate full
steam ahead.

I went to Italy with William Trevor in *My House in Umbria,* where I saw "a yellowish building at the end of a track . . .
curving through a landscape of olive trees and cypresses . . .
broom and laburnum daub the clover slopes, poppies and ge-
raniums sprinkle the meadows. . . . The hill continues to rise
gently, and there's a field of sunflowers."

"Mom!" George's voice cuts into my reading, pulling me
back to the here and now. "What's for dinner?"

Hmmm? "Pasta, I think . . . just drizzled with a bit of olive oil." I shut the door to my music room, and I'm back in Umbria.

Traveling by steel ship, I crossed an ocean to reach Nigeria in J. M. G. Le Clézio's *Onitsha*. It was a rough journey: "Day after day, only this hard sea, the air moving at the speed of the ship, the slow path of the sun across the steel walls, its glare bearing down upon forehead and chest, burning deep inside." But oh, what I saw when I got there: "At sunset the sky darkened to the west. . . . Downstream the river inscribed a slow curving line to the south, as vast as an arm of the sea, with the hesitant traces of small islands, like rafts adrift. The storm swirled. There were bloodied streaks in the sky, gaps in the clouds. Then, very rapidly, the black cloud went back up the river, chasing before it the flying ibises still lit by the sun."

I woke to take a midnight walk in Ireland in Claire Keegan's short story "Walk the Blue Fields": "The blue night has spread itself darkly over the fields . . . spring has come, dry and promising. The alder is shooting out, her pale limbs brazen. . . . All around the air is sharp with the tang of wild currant bushes. A lamb climbs out of a deep sleep and walks across the blue field. Overhead, the stars have rolled into place." I've always wanted to go to Ireland, having read and reread Yeats all those years during college and beyond, and now I've been.

In "The Lake Isle of Innisfree," Yeats writes,

> *And I shall have some peace there, for peace comes dropping*
> *slow,*
> *Dropping from the veils of the morning to where the cricket*
> *sings;*
> *There midnight's all a glimmer, and noon a purple glow,*
> *And evening full of the linnet's wings.*

This was one of my favorite poems because it reminded me of where I grew up, beside a lake, but also offered something new and different, the seclusion of a small cabin, "of clay and wattles made." What the heck was a wattle? It didn't matter to me. I just wanted to live again by the shore, and to live for the first time in a small cabin beside "bean-rows" and a "hive for the honey bee," to be where the crickets sing (I knew that sound well) and the evening is "full of linnet's wings."

Linnet? Again, no idea, but I was seduced. The mixture of the familiar and the new was intoxicating.

But I also wanted what was old and long gone. Having lost my sister, my craving to go backward in time, to revisit when she'd been alive, had grown stronger. I wanted to take a vacation to the Evanston of our childhood. I'd choose summertime, when we girls were allowed to stay up late and we spent our evenings outside, playing tag and hide-and-seek and dodgeball with the neighborhood kids. When we became tired of running around, we just dropped, falling into a heap of children lolling on the grass. When we felt hungry, the older kids, like Anne-Marie, organized the younger ones to go back into houses, retrieving popsicles or peaches, or even better yet, money for the approaching ice-cream truck.

The gassy smell of the truck and its loud jingle taped to replay over and over came long before the sight of the truck itself, farting down the street with ice-cream cones and sandwiches and bars. After eating our ice-cream bars my sisters and I stayed outside, sitting on the front steps until our parents called us in. Fireflies skirted over the lawn and into the bushes and trees. We never talked about what we would do when we grew up. Sitting together under the open night sky, watching the fireflies light up and go dark, then light up again, there was no question that we would do whatever we wanted to do. Anything was possible.

I went back to that place and those feelings when I read Kevin Canty's story "Burning Bridges, Breaking Glass" from his collection *Where the Money Went*. Although the plot of the story revolves around an older man and his affair with a younger woman, the background is pure midwestern fecundity, the wild fertility of possibility offered by long evenings and huge open spaces and endless starlit skies. Canty writes about "the perfume of a Midwestern spring, gasoline and rose and tar, the sounds of people gunning it in the distance, the constant hiss of the interstate, the sounds of breaking glass and laughter, the sound of life itself." For me, it was summer, not spring, when I heard those sounds and smelled those smells, and the story pulled me back into childhood.

The narrator in "Burning Bridges, Breaking Glass" feels the same pull backward. He is a middle-aged man with an alcohol problem, trying to put an end to his drinking by spending two weeks at an expensive spa in the desert. There he meets Karen, the wife of a doctor. He falls in love with her, and after she leaves, he decides to follow her home to Ohio.

Rossbach finds Karen in Ohio, but more important, he rediscovers the place and time of his youth, the "full glorious spring with flowers bursting out of driveway beds and bees everywhere." I become exhilarated by the background of a midwestern spring, just as Rossbach finds himself entranced with the same phenomenon. As he began recovering evidence of his childhood, the "pink-and-purple spring he had forgotten," so did I.

Rossbach immerses himself in "the bright bee-loud afternoon of full spring" where "cherry trees in the parking lot blossomed in pink, snowing pink and white petals onto the cars parked beneath them." Remembering those "days at seventeen of just feeling himself in his body, the spring of it, the miracle," Rossbach feels "the green fuse still lit in him, the spark": possibility in his life has been reignited.

I finished reading that story with my own "green fuse lit," my own youth recovered. I remembered lying in bed at night with the windows opened to let in the warm summer air. From the bed, I could hear the traffic on Golf Road and the radio playing on the neighbor's porch. I smelled the dankness of freshly turned earth in our garden, the sweet scent of cut grass, and the smoky smell of barbecues. The smells and sounds were like an invitation to me, a summons to run out and join the universe. I was older then, beyond hide-and-seek games and waiting for the ice-cream truck, but I still believed my future was limitless. I knew that the breeze coming in from the window was full of promises of adventure and love and fun, promises just waiting to be fulfilled.

Books were my time machine, my vehicles of recovery and reignited bliss from childhood and beyond. Knut Hamsun's *Dreamers* brought me back to college, and to the spring evenings when I found myself embracing a newly beloved male beneath a flowering tree. Hamsun renders the hormonal fever of spring in all its bewildering power: "It was spring again. And spring was almost unbearable for sensitive hearts. It drove creation to its utmost limits, it wafted its spice-laden breath even into the nostrils of the innocent."

Dreamers is set in a small town on the Norwegian coast around the turn of the century. After being pent up all winter, the citizens of this coastal town let loose under the winds rolling in off the sea, liberated by the smells of warming soil and budding trees and blooming flowers. The characters in *Dreamers* indulge in lusty dreams of love and fortune, desire born out of sudden sun and heat: "It was weather for dreams; for little fluttering quests of the heart. . . . From every rocky islet came the calling of birds . . . and the seal thrust up its dripping head from the water, looked round, and dived again down to its own world below."

Emotions and desires settle down as spring turns to summer: "Corn and potatoes growing; and meadows waving; herring stored in every shed, cows and goats milking full pails, and rolling in fat themselves." There is a bountiful supply of food, and of dreams as well: "Summer is the time for dreaming, and then you have to stop. But some people go on dreaming all their lives, and cannot change."

Lucky people, to dream all their lives. A certain profound optimism is required: the belief that dreams can come true. And I realized there was yet another reason for me to be on my reading quest. To get back to that place where I was sure of all my dreams. The smell of the grass, the stars heavy in the humid sky, the warm brush of air against my cheek, all were embedded into my brain. The memories lined up as a fence, and I was safe in the enclosure. I was ten years old, and all my tomorrows waited, a whole world just for me. Or I was eighteen years old again, kissing under a budding apple tree and sure that my whole life would always be filled with the same intensity of desire and intention.

After I read *Dreamers*, my mother told me that Knut Hamsun had been a favorite author of my grandfather. I was delighted to hear it. I shared Hamsun now with my grandfather, a man I hadn't known well but whom I loved. I wondered what escape he found when reading Hamsun. I pictured my grandfather sitting in a white cane lawn chair in a patch of sun before a drift of spring green trees. The scent of white lilac bushes floats toward him over the grass. He never could have imagined a granddaughter of his reading Hamsun in a cat-stinky purple chair in Connecticut beside a window wide open to summer breezes. Two readers caught up by the place and season of one book, for very different reasons but with the same result: a love of the story told, and the comfort of the place offered, a place in time and in the world. An escape, a vacation, a recovering of memories. Travel did not have to be solitary. A book shared was an escape with company.

Even when I read a book where the story had nothing to do with an experience of my own, I found resonance from recovered memories, and an escape from the present. In "The Loneliness of the Long-distance Runner," a short story by Alan Sillitoe, a boy is sent to a Borstal, an English reform school for delinquents. Our boy Smith has been very delinquent, robbing a local bakeshop and hiding the money in an old drainpipe just outside the ramshackle house he shares with his family. He'd turned to robbery in an effort to recapture the brief moment of bliss his family experienced upon receiving the death benefits of his father: "I'd never known a family as happy as ours was in that couple of months when we'd got all the money we needed." When a terrible rain releases the stolen money right in front of an investigating copper, Smith is sent off to the Borstal.

But life isn't all bad in the reform school. Smith is recruited for the cross-country team and set to train for a countrywide competition. His early-morning runs out into the countryside provide him with both solitude and escape, and he looks forward to them as the best part of his day.

I had nothing in common with the Smith boy, and yet in his description of the early-morning runs, I recovered a very distinct memory of an early-morning walk I took in my late twenties. I was at an environmental conference in the Adirondacks, staying in a farmhouse about three miles down the road from the conference center. After the first day of meetings, excited about everything we were going to accomplish in the coming months, I headed back to my farmhouse for a good night's sleep.

During the night the weather turned very cold, and in the unheated upper room of the farmhouse, I slept badly. Even wrapping myself up in all my clothes, I could not get warm. Finally I just got out of bed. I headed out into the last darkness of the night, the air frosty and still all around me. If I was going to be cold, I'd rather be outside, moving around, than shivering in a narrow hard bed.

As I walked, the sky began to lighten over the far mountains. The sun rose before me, doling out sunlight in strips along the frost-whitened grass. I walked in gravel that broke like ice beneath my shoes, and fall grasshoppers, released by the coming warmth of the sun, jumped before me, guiding my way. As I walked, I noticed everything around me. The flattened grass glinting under the sun. The bordering bushes sparked red with color. The trees, black and stark against the sky, and the mountains beyond, purple under a haze of pink and apricot. The fresh air pricked against my cheeks, and I took breath into my lungs in big gulps. I felt as if I could fly, borne away up into the mountains by the pure energy coming up from the awakening ground and racing now through my veins.

I was just like the Borstal boy, running out in the morning, the world fresh and open all around him: "As soon as I take that first flying leap out into the frosty grass of an early morning when even birds haven't the heart to whistle, I get to thinking and that's what I like. . . . Sometimes I think that I've never been so free as during that couple of hours when I'm trotting up the path out of the gates and turning by that bare-faced, big-bellied oak tree at the lane end." I recognized that feeling of "never been so free"—that was how I felt that morning in the Adirondacks.

To go back in time was to return to when I felt optimistic and unbounded, back before my sister died. Everyone has a before and after, the times of our lives divided by an event of loss or suffering or hardship. For me, the event was the death of my sister, unexpected and too soon. In the months after Anne-Marie died, I lost all faith in the future. I took my sister's death as a sign that the whole world no longer waited for me.

But I was wrong. Through this year of reading I was recovering that "green fuse still lit" of possibility. Not only were books carrying me away on escapades of new experiences but the people and places and atmospheres created by authors were also bringing me back to those times in my life where I looked forward to tomorrow.

How to live? Engaged in the present but willing to take vacations to other places and other times. My future depended on it. We all need to escape once in a while, from the big and little pressures, heartaches, and disappointments of daily life. I need to escape from the place where Anne-Marie no longer lived, and go back to when we were both alive, back to when what lay ahead seemed endless and wonderful.

Books are the frigate to wherever I want to go. My future is not infinite, I know that now. But my life is as full of possibility as it had been when I was just a girl, sitting out on the front steps with my sisters, eating ice cream and watching the fireflies flicker on and off over the darkened lawn.

18

**THE
ANSWERS
THAT
MYSTERIES
PROVIDE**

*I realized it was my decision whether I would
interpret the ending as unjust and unsatisfactory
and suffer because of it or decided that this, and
only this, was the fitting ending.*

BERNHARD SCHLINK,
Self's Murder

I CAN SEE IT NOW: A YELLOW HAT FLOATING ON WATER,
brown hair spreading out all around. I first read *The Scarlet
Ruse* by John D. MacDonald thirty years ago, and I still remember how Travis McGee had cut the hair himself, shearing
the woman and then attaching her lost locks to the hat. The hat
was flung out into the bay, creating an illusion to capture the
bad guys. "It was better than I hoped. It was spooking her. She
floated out there, dead in a raft. I wondered if she had ever really been able to comprehend the fact of her own eventual and
inevitable death. Today, my friends, we each have one day less,
every one of us. And joy is the only thing that slows the clock."

Wisdom from a mystery, one in a series of twenty-one
color-coded books written by MacDonald, every one of them
read by my father and most of them by me too, over the course
of the long, hot, humid days and nights of Chicago summers.

A book doesn't have to be part of the canon of great literature to make a difference in the reader's life. I was seventeen
when I first read MacDonald's line "Joy is the only thing that
slows the clock." The underlying avowal of letting go of misery and exulting in rapture, big and small, is more relevant to

me now than it was then, but even back then it sparked something in me, and it stuck with me. Not only because it was from a MacDonald mystery, and reading MacDonald was an addiction I shared with my father, but because mysteries as a genre have something to say to all of us about the world, and our efforts to make sense of our place in it.

Growing up, everyone in my family read mysteries. Especially in the summer, we worked our way through volumes of murders, disappearances, and other acts of treachery and deception. There was nothing better than being the last ones still on the beach, panting our ways through gripping stories of twists and turns. My father spent his summers with the two Macs: John D. MacDonald and his Travis McGee novels and Ross Macdonald and his Lew Archer series. My mother preferred Rex Stout and P. D. James, Anne-Marie loved Agatha Christie, and Natasha was devoted to Dorothy L. Sayers's Lord Peter Wimsey. I started early on with the racecourse mysteries of Dick Francis and kept pace with my father's appetite for MacDonald and Macdonald.

The first summer I spent working in New York City, Anne-Marie gave me an open invitation to come out to the house in Bellport. After a seventy-hour workweek, weeks at a time, it was bliss, when a break finally came, to head out of the sticky, greasy heat of a New York City summer and arrive in the salty, breezy air of eastern Long Island. I arrived carrying nothing more than a swimsuit and a pair of shorts. Anne-Marie provided everything else I needed, from suntan lotion to my own room at the top of the house. The room was empty but for a twin bed with a green-and-white comforter faded with washings, a spiderweb-decorated floor lamp, and a woven basket filled with *New York* magazines going back to the 1970s.

My first weekend out there, I found a treasure trove of

mysteries. One floor below my attic room was Anne-Marie's office, a space lined with books. One side was all academic books, treatises on architecture, tomes of philosophy, and journals on art history and critical theory. The other side of the room was lined with narrow shelves tightly filled with novels, poetry collections—and mysteries. I reread my way through works of Agatha Christie, volume after volume, during that first summer as a New Yorker.

Even before they could read, Anne-Marie started my kids on the summer mystery tradition. She sat with them out on the porch in Bellport, translating all her Tintin books by Hergé from French to English, thrilling them with *The Castafiore Emerald*, *The Blue Lotus*, and *The Black Island*. When they got older, she would walk with the boys over to the Bellport library. There they would wander together through the children's stacks. Using Anne-Marie's library card (which I still have in my wallet—light blue with the navy logo of a seagull standing on a pile of books), they checked out Nate the Great mysteries by Marjorie Weinman Sharmat and Elizabeth Levy's Something Queer mysteries.

The first summer after Anne-Marie died, the boys, Jack, and I went out to Bellport to visit Marvin. Pulling up into the gravel driveway out back, I realized that I expected to see Anne-Marie coming across the grass to meet us as we disgorged from our car. But of course she didn't. She was gone; we had scattered her ashes the month before off Bellport's beach on Fire Island. How could I come out to this house without her waiting there for me? I stayed in the car as the boys tumbled out and made their own way across the grass, banging in through the back screen door, shouting out for Marvin.

I finally got out of the car that day and went inside to join everyone else. During the afternoon we spent there, I went up to Anne-Marie's office and ran my hand over the row of Agatha Christies. I reached for *Ten Little Indians*, then put it back. I wasn't ready yet to reread a book I'd shared with my sister. I sat in the old gray chair facing west over the hedge planted just a few years earlier and already growing high, and I cried.

Since that summer, we've gone out every year to Bellport, and every year I still get the feeling that *this* year, Anne-Marie will come out across the grass to meet us. It's a fleeting sensation, one moment of insanity against the reality of what I know, but for that one moment, the possibility of her crossing over the grass in her black sandals, short khaki shorts, and white T-shirt makes more sense to me than her death ever will. In my internal universe, the order I seek is one in which she plays a prominent and constant role. No other world rings true for me.

It is that search for order that drives my hunger for reading mysteries. Sure, I find sparks of wisdom in a good mystery, but what I am really looking for are solutions. I'm searching for an order in the universe. In a world where, sometimes, very little makes sense, a mystery can take the twists and turns of life and run them through a plot that eventually *does* make sense. A solution to a question is found. The sense of satisfaction is huge.

Owing to this summer of my reading a book a day, our yearly trip out to Bellport would be only for a short visit, enough time for lunch and an afternoon spent at the beach. When we arrived, I once again stayed in the car for a moment, while the boys and Jack made their way across the grass and into the house. I waited in anticipation, but Anne-Marie didn't come. No matter how many summers I returned, and no matter how long I stayed in the car, Anne-Marie was not going to come out and greet me with smiles and kisses. I waited for just another moment, and then I went to join the others in the house.

We went out to Fire Island that afternoon, traveling across

the Great South Bay in Marvin's speedboat. It was a hot day and very windy, with huge waves coming up onto the shores of Fire Island. Too rough for me to swim, and anyway, I preferred to read under the umbrella. How wonderful this year to have an excuse—"I have to finish today's book!" I opened my book, a mystery by Bernhard Schlink called *Self's Murder*, and began reading. Schlink is most famous for his novel *The Reader*, but this mystery of his quickly drew me in.

The main character in *Self's Murder* is private investigator Gerhard Self, former state prosecutor under the Nazis and current do-gooder. As a private eye, Self is trying hard to right his past wrongs in a self-imposed penance of diligent work. Over seventy years of age, he is well aware that most potential clients "will be more impressed by a younger fellow with a cell phone and a BMW who's a former cop . . . than by an old guy driving an old Opel." Nevertheless, Self is not ready to call it quits. He struggles on, caring for those who have come to him for help and struggling to accept that there are times when there is nothing he can do for them: "I was tortured by the powerlessness of not being able to do anything anymore, not being able to fix things."

There was a sudden interruption to my reading.

"Mom! Don't you want to go bodysurfing?" Peter called from the water.

"Not today, honey, I am loving this book."

Self agrees to take on a new case, helping the director of a bank find the real identity of one of its silent partners. The search takes unexpected turns, going back in time to the plundering of Jewish property under the Nazis, and forward again through the present-day strife of a unified Germany, with its problems of resurgent Nazi skinheads and the integration of the East Germans into a Western mentality and culture.

In the end, Self solves the mystery of the identity of the silent partner, while also uncovering a connected plot of deception and thievery that has led to a series of murders. But he can't prove what he knows about the murders, and the perpetrator never has to pay for his crimes.

Self feels cheated. He has solved the case of the murders, but been denied the satisfaction of justice served. Self comes to understand then that his own sanity depends upon his accepting what he cannot change: "I realized it was my decision whether I would interpret the ending as unjust and unsatisfactory and suffer because of it or decided that this, and only this, was the fitting ending."

Wisdom from a mystery, discovered on a beach. And a new understanding of order in the universe. We cannot control events around us, but we are responsible for our reactions to those events. I was responsible for how I reacted to the death of my sister. Once past the initial shock of losing her and the period of grief that followed, I could choose how to respond.

I tuned in to what was going on around me on the beach. Michael, who had a healthy fear of waves after one year's bodysurfing mishap resulted in a trip to the ER and twenty stitches across his lip, was building a castle in the sand, while Martin dug out the moat and connecting canal leading down into the water. Peter and Jack were bodysurfing, and George sat beside me, reading. Marvin and Dorothy, the woman who would become his wife, were taking a walk down the beach.

Peter ran up from the water. "Got anything to drink, Mom?"

"I'm hungry," yelled Michael. I turned to the cooler and pulled out bottles of water and bunches of grapes.

"What time are we leaving?" asked George, never one for prolonged exposure to heat or sun.

"Anytime is fine with me," I said.

Anytime was fine, anything was fine, everything was fine. My response was up to me. The fitting ending is determined by *how* a person takes what life gives them, not by *what* life gives them.

But what about what life takes away? How to live with the loss of my sister. How to live. That response was wholly up to me as well.

Mysteries tell me there is order in the universe. And I believe that there is. But a good whodunit also demonstrates that for some questions, there is no answer. I know that to be true as well. We all face mysteries—*Why did that have to happen?*—that we will never be able to understand. But we can, and we do, find *order* somewhere, whether it be in our books, our friends, our family, or our faith. Order is defined by how we live our lives. Order is created by how we respond to what life dishes out to us. Order is found in accepting that not all questions can be answered.

On that beautiful August afternoon, I sat back in my beach chair and surveyed where I was. Looking over a glittering ocean under a blue sky. Kids close by me on the sand, Jack still jumping the waves, Marvin and Dorothy coming back now over the dunes. I was doing okay. I was creating order by following lessons learned from the books I immersed myself in, day after day. My year of magical reading was proving to be a fitting ending to my overwhelming sorrow and a solid beginning to the rest of my life.

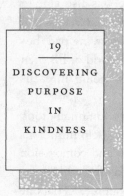

19

DISCOVERING

PURPOSE

IN

KINDNESS

Acts of kindness demonstrate, in the clearest
possible way, that we are vulnerable and
dependent animals who have no better resource
than each other.

ADAM PHILLIPS AND

BARBARA TAYLOR,

On Kindness

EARLY IN SEPTEMBER, MY STEPDAUGHTER, MEREDITH, CALLED from London. She'd moved to England eight months earlier, but the planned future with her boyfriend hadn't worked out. In the predawn hours of a Thursday morning, I reached for the ringing phone and found her on the other end, weeping and overwhelmed. Jack took the phone from me and told Meredith to get on a plane. He mouthed an "Okay?" to me, and I nodded.

What else could I do? How else to respond to despair but with kindness and a place to live safe and protected, for as long as she wanted? It is my first impulse, to offer solace or comfort, no matter how small, to a person who is sad and confused. I couldn't solve Meredith's problem. But I could be witness to her grief, and a companion through the hardship.

In the graphic memoir *Stitches*, author David Small tells the story of his childhood. His early years, living with a depressed mother and a detached father and spending summers with a psychotic grandmother, were marked by verbal abuse and utter lack of physical affection. Stricken with a throat cancer caused by his father giving him radiation to cure respiratory problems, Small was literally and figuratively mute for years. He turned to art to express himself. Through his art he was also able to find relief from the prevailing misery in his home. One page in *Stitches* shows a young Small diving into his drawing pad, being taken down through the page and into a world of his own creation, a world safe for being his own, and for being unreachable by his family.

It was only when he was a teenager that an adult finally took notice of Small's desolation and reached out to help him. This man, a therapist, showed Small the kindness and compassion the boy had been missing in his life. "He treated me like a favorite son," Small writes. "He truly cared about me." That one caring adult, and the sanctuary of his art, led Small past the misery of his childhood and into a fulfilling life.

In *On Kindness* by Adam Phillips and Barbara Taylor, the authors argue that human kindness *is* human nature: "History shows us the manifold expressions of humanity's desire to connect, from classical celebrations of friendship, to Christian teachings on love and charity, to twentieth-century philosophies of social welfare." Phillips and Taylor believe that in lightening the burdens of others—easing their fears and fostering their hopes—we gain strength. And when that same kindness is given back to us, we flourish, our own fears lessened and our own hopes bolstered: "Kindness . . . creates the kind of intimacy, the kind of involvement with other people that we both fear and crave . . . kindness, fundamentally, makes life worth living."

My four boys were excited that their sister, Meredith, was coming home. They didn't ask why she was leaving London or inquire as to the circumstances of her changed life. In fact, the only question they asked at all was if her name would be added to the rota for dinner cleanup. Yes, it would be. Nothing like chores and routine to get a person back on track. Friday evening, Jack picked up Meredith and her two bulging suitcases at JFK and brought her back to Westport. We all settled in, seven at home again.

I expect acts of kindness within my family, physical and verbal demonstrations of acceptance and support from one member to another. We have our share of spats between siblings (and parents), but nevertheless, our home is the place where we all can be just who we are and expect to be loved for exactly that. It is this underlying unconditional love that makes the family unit a refuge, and the family house a place to return to for solace and peace at the end of a school day or workday—or after a boyfriend and a future planned around him go down the tubes.

Outside the family unit, my experience is that kindness between friends, acquaintances, and even strangers is the rule rather than the exception. After my sister died, I was buffeted by acts of kindness from friends. People wrote cards, made dinners, brought flowers. One friend planted a lilac bush in my garden, placing it so I can see it whenever I am in the kitchen. The bush has grown large, and in the spring it is heavy with dark, fragrant buds. I think of Anne-Marie every time I see the flowers, and I think of my friend Heather, who planted it for me.

I grew up on stories of generosity and compassion. Some families thrive on war stories of valor and bravery, and other families draw strength from a past of pioneering and privation. In my family's mythology, kindness is the greatest power. There were the stories of wartime kindness, like how the couple in Regensburg who, after losing all three sons to war, took my father in to live with them; or how after the war the entire population of my great-grandmother's village outside

Antwerp came out to pray for penicillin to be delivered to their local doctor. Within days a convoy of American soldiers delivered the medicine, and the certain death of a tooth-abscessed man was averted.

There were the funny stories too. One of my father's responsibilities as a young boy was to herd the family sheep out to the fields in the morning. While out tending the sheep one day, my father was bitten on the leg by a stray dog. It was a deep bite, and my father began to bleed. An old babushka approached him across the field and offered to help. My father was grateful for her offer. His leg hurt, and the bleeding wouldn't stop. Then the old woman explained *how* she could help. She'd pull up her skirt and, stooping over his bitten leg, urinate on the broken skin to disinfect the wound. She gestured to a group of boys coming over the hill, all friends of my father. He hadn't seen them coming.

"I can pee on you, but with the other boys around, maybe you'd rather I wouldn't?"

My father nodded.

"Then run on home, and wash your leg up with soap. Go!"

The babushka offered kindness both ways, to pee or not to pee, and my father made his choice. He still bears the scar of that bite on his leg, but the way he explains it, if his friends had seen him pissed on by a local grandmother, the mental scars would have been much worse.

My grandmother in Belgium started up a charity during the war. Its purpose? To darn the socks of families deprived of maids during the war. After the war, she devoted her knitting to the "poor children of the Congo." Why children living in the heat of central Africa would need woolens was beyond me, but her heart was in the right place, and her mind was subconsciously trying to somehow make up for the horrors King Leopold II had exercised while governing the Belgian Congo.

That same grandmother was the only one in her family to welcome home a cousin who had left for Africa as a priest and came back as a husband to an African woman and father to three mixed-race children. "All love is sacred" was my grandmother's philosophy, and she helped the young family settle in to life in provincial Belgium.

My uncle George's philosophy was to keep loved ones fed, at all costs. In Germany after the war, food was hard to find. Uncle George kept my father fed despite the shortages. He worked in the kitchens of the American army barracks and sneaked out sausages and hams to my father, food that kept him alive until he was enrolled in the University of Regensburg and taken in by the German couple. Even then, my uncle kept passing on food to my father to share with his new family, as thanks to the couple for taking my father in.

Uncle George worked for the Americans for another thirty years, ending up as the head cook at an American base along the Czech border. He was let go when the Americans caught him taking sausages for his Sunday lunch. "But I've been taking sausages for thirty years!" he exclaimed. The Americans wanted to keep him on—he was a great cook, a cheerful fellow, and nice to everyone—but rules were rules. So Uncle George began working at a bar in the local village, a bar that quickly became the favorite watering hole for off-duty GIs, including the men who had to fire him from their kitchen. My sisters and I understood the lesson taught: kindness sometimes operates outside of the law, but in the end, kindness overrides even the most law bidden.

I wanted to do something to show Meredith that I cared for

her and cared about what happened to her. Yet she had no visible wounds that needed disinfecting and no socks that needed darning. I wasn't one for praying, but I did try to make her favorite dishes for dinner, frying up a sausage or two in honor of Uncle George. In *On Kindness*, the writers note that "acts of kindness demonstrate, in the clearest possible way, that we are vulnerable and dependent animals who have no better resource than each other." I wanted to be a resource for Meredith, but what kind? *On Kindness* makes much of the caring instinct that exists between parents and child: "Between parents and children . . . kindness is expected, sanctioned, and indeed obligatory." But I was not Meredith's parent; I was not her pal; I was not her aunt or grandmother; I was not her babysitter or teacher.

Meredith and I have not always had the easiest of relationships. She was the only daughter of Jack, and I was the opinionated second wife. There were plenty of occasions for us to clash. One of the very first times Jack, Meredith, and I went out together was a Sunday trip to Bear Mountain, a state park close to New York City. It was late October, the leaves almost gone from the trees, but the temperature was warm, with clear skies and bright sun overhead. We spent the day doing little kid things—playing on a playground, taking a hike around the pond, and running a tag game on the park's patchy grass fields.

On the drive back to Meredith's home in New Jersey, where she lived then with her mother, Meredith began to complain that she had to sit in the backseat.

"Should we just drop Nina off here, Meredith?" Jack asked. "Get you up in the front?" We were on Route 9 at the time, somewhere in the suburbs of Bergen County. Night had fallen, and the temperature had turned chilly.

"Yes, Dad. Let her out here."

Jack laughed, and slowed the car down.

"What are you doing?" I asked.

Jack winked at me. "Are you sure, Meredith? It's awfully cold and a very long walk back to the city."

"Do it, Dad, she'll be fine."

Jack did not "do it"; he sped up again, and we drove Meredith home to her mother.

I suppose the best way to define our relationship is that I am Meredith's oldest friend. I've known her since she was six years old; I've traveled with her and lived with her. We share a love of cats and horses, and of red wine and chocolate. She's held me when I've cried, and I've held her when she needed me. As all long friendships do, our relationship has flowered and blundered, steamed ahead and stuttered to a stop, then restarted itself again. And as is true in all friendships, the restart always comes from an act of kindness. The weekend after our trip to Bear Mountain, I let Meredith sit in the front seat of our rented car. When Jack moved into my Chelsea apartment, I welcomed Meredith with a day of baking Christmas cookies shaped as cats. The cookies came out of the oven hard as a rock, so we used them as ornaments for the Christmas tree. We pounded a hole through the top of each cookie with a nail (yes, they were that hard) and laced ribbons through for hanging on branches.

When Meredith moved in with us full-time nine years later, forbearance was offered on her part by how she treated her younger brothers. She was exceptionally patient with them, and affectionate. On my part, I insisted to Jack that we give up our bedroom in the two-bedroom apartment and move out to the living room. I knew that Meredith needed her privacy and her own space.

Thirteen years later, she needed space and privacy and a safe haven all over again. I could do that, easily. But I wanted to do more for her. Love between a mother and child is expected. My love for Meredith has to be re-proved, again and again. Big act or small, I wanted to do something special. I offered to take her to the U.S. Open tennis tournament in Queens, and she took me up on it.

"It will mean getting up really early," I cautioned her. Every year I buy grounds admission tickets for the Open. Grounds admission means no reserved seats were waiting for me. But by getting out to the tennis center by 8:00 a.m. and waiting in line for the gates to open at ten, and then running as fast as I could to the Grandstand Stadium (which had only nonreserved seating), I could snag front-row seats for the day. If I knocked a few people down along the way, I apologized (kindness) and kept going (determination: this was, after all, the one and only U.S. Open). I explained the plan to Meredith and she was up for it.

We got to Flushing Meadows in plenty of time, with only a few people before us in line. I got out my reading for the day, *Better* by John O'Brien. It was a depressing novel about sex, drinking, and money. The book has more than a few graphic scenes of alcohol-fueled sex and debauchery integral to the plot, and I hunched over as I read, hoping no one was peeking over my shoulder. At ten the gates opened and I took off at a gallop, climbing the steps up into the grandstand two at a time and then sliding into front-row seats behind the baseline and slightly to the right. Meredith came in behind me and smiled.

"These are great seats," she said.

"Yes, yes," agreed the panting couple taking the seats beside us. Their faces were decorated with red and white paint, colored in to look like the Danish flag across their foreheads and cheeks.

"We're here for Caroline Wozniacki," said the man who had come in to sit behind us. "Who are you here for?"

I turned around to talk. "Who is playing the grandstand today?"

"Tommy Haas, Kim Clijsters, Wozniacki . . . Serena and Venus are supposed to be playing doubles here later." Meredith and I looked at each other and did the high five. The Williams sisters? Then Meredith went off in search of coffee while I turned back to finish *Better*. We still had an hour to go before the matches began.

O'Brien is best known for his book about a self-destructing alcoholic, *Leaving Las Vegas*. *Better* is also about characters seeking oblivion and release in alcohol. A wealthy man named Double Felix runs his home as an open house for alcoholic males and for women willing to provide sex in exchange for a privileged lifestyle. William is the narrator, a previously ambitious young man who has been sucked into the narcotic atmosphere of the house, reveling in sex and alcohol round the clock. Most mornings begin with him slinging back vodka with his host Double Felix, and the drinking continues all day long. What O'Brien does so well in his novels about alcoholics is in how he exposes the apathy behind alcoholism, the giving up on life and the utter deterioration of will. His characters rely on inebriation to remain sedated through the stages of their self-destruction. William is never fully present for anything. All is hazed and clouded by drinking.

When William finally moved out of his stupor and acted to save one person and then protect another, I was startled. The book had changed tempo on me. O'Brien was offering his character a chance to restart his life. I read on with renewed interest as William took that chance and moved beyond apathy and into engagement. He comes out of his fugue state and into a state of hope and possibility: "Part of my enthusiasm, such as it is, for whatever turn my life is taking is the need to assert it all over the place in as many ways as possible." Assertion is a step in the right direction, a positive movement forward. He takes that first step forward by caring for the people around him.

"Be kind," Plato said, "for everyone you meet is fighting a hard battle." Kindness is a positive and vigorous force to make a connection across a divide. William is alone in his inebriation, but when he reaches out to help the former prostitute who actually cares for him, he is no longer alone. When I was devastated by the death of my sister, the words and letters and hugs of friends reminded me that I was not isolated in my grief but surrounded by people who cared about me. When Meredith came home from London, she found her brothers, her father, and me with our arms wide open. All these situations are different in circumstances but alike in the kindness that bridges the divide between one person and another.

There is no way to balance the scale of inequities, and I can't find any persuasive explanation for why illness, death, and hardship are so inequitably distributed. But I do find that sympathy, compassion, and solicitude are an answer to the consequences of pain and sorrow. Jane Kenyon writes in her poem "Killing the Plants," "They will go on giving / alms to the poor: sweet air, miraculous / flowers, the example of persistence." Kindness *is* persistence; it demonstrates an unyielding will to answer the unanswerable questions of tragedy and loss. In the face of hardship, compassion answers back with stores of relief. Even the most generous of acts can never bring Anne-Marie back to me, but each gentle act of caring relieves the weight of the battle, lightens my load, and offers strength of support.

Now it was my turn to offer Meredith the strength and persistence of my support and caring. I gave her a day away from her troubles, a day off from thinking about her future. I gave both of us a beautiful sunny day spent drinking lemonade, watching tennis, and laughing and cheering along with the crowds. The Williams sisters played and won and wowed us with their presence. Kim Clijsters won, and Wozniacki won. I can't remember if Tommy Haas won, but who cared: he looked gorgeous. Meredith and I giggled together when he changed shirts, exposing his tanned chest.

Over the years, the incident of Meredith and me and Jack speeding home from Bear Mountain, and Meredith wanting to leave me on the side of the road, has become a family joke. But I think the core of the story is serious. It is the question of who was to be kept safe in the car and who could be let go. Who would be treated with kindness and who would be left alone on the highway. I wanted to reassure Meredith then, and now, that kindness is a strength, that acts of kindness are lines passed back and forth between people to form a web of safety. I want her to know that she will always have a place in the car, in the house, in the family. And good seats at the Open, if she is willing to get up early and run for them.

Read anything, as long as you can't wait to pick
it up again.

NICK HORNBY,
Housekeeping vs. the Dirt

MY YEAR OF READING WAS COMING TO AN END.

"You must be so ready to just *relax*," a friend said to me.

But I was relaxed. A year of pleasure had been afforded to me. A year of books. No matter how burdensome other aspects of my life became, the driving and the cooking and the laundry, reading my daily book was always a joy. I hadn't been sick one day during my entire year of reading. Bathed in pleasure, I was immune to illness. People who didn't know me well told me I'd be off books for sure once the new year was rung in. Ha! I was as hooked as ever on the pleasure of reading.

Book bliss, brought on by good writing. If I didn't like a book within the first ten pages or so, I put it away and chose another one from my shelf of waiting tomes. As Nick Hornby counseled me, way back in February, in his book *Housekeeping vs. the Dirt*, "One of the problems, it seems to me, is that we have got it into our heads that books should be hard work, and that unless they're hard work, they're not doing us any good." But all the books I read, the hard ones to work through and the easy ones to devour, were doing me good, lots of good. And bringing me pleasure, lots of pleasure.

I didn't need earth-moving writing to become hooked on a book. I just needed a good story, intriguing characters, interesting background. Sure, I loved the profoundly moving literature of Paul Auster and Muriel Barbery and Chris Cleave, but satisfaction came in simpler packages as well. Like the *Sunday Philosophy Club*, the first in the Isabel Dalhousie series written by Alexander McCall Smith. I fell in love with Isabel Dalhousie, the main character in McCall Smith's series, and my fascination with her was enough to keep me in my chair, reading up on her latest adventures in modern-day Edinburgh.

Isabel is extremely thoughtful and kind, yet capable of snarls of impatience or jealousy. She is interested in art and music but even more curious about the personalities of artists, musicians, and anyone else she meets. She feels obligated to help others and to connect to others, yet she is no pushover. Quite willing to state her own opinions strongly, she is also open-minded enough to change her views when presented with strong arguments. She is smart and funny, and, despite her very serious nature when it comes to questions of moral philosophy, she never takes herself too seriously. Isabel is not necessarily a very real or deeply probed character—nor are any of the characters in Smith's books—but she is a comforting one and an appealing one, a brainy do-gooder, an optimistic and compassionate heroine.

I'd also been captivated by Isabel's lifestyle. I'd happily take on her full-time housekeeper; her comfy town house filled with books and art; her lush garden complete with a fox and overgrown rhododendrons; her job editing a journal devoted to the philosophy of applied ethics (i.e., whether and how to be a good person); and her money. She has scads of it, plenty to live very comfortably and yet not so much that the money becomes a burden.

I read McCall Smith's sixth installment, *The Lost Art of Gratitude*, on the first day of October. Mixed in with a plot about financial fraud, plagiarism, and the changing relationship with the father of her child, Isabel pontificates on the nature of gratitude, as when she recognized that birthplace "determined what we were . . . a culture, a language, a set of genes determining complexion, height, susceptibility to disease," and that we ought to feel grateful for what our chance of birthplace brought to us. I agreed with her ruminations that from those who had been given much in terms of health and wealth and security, much might be expected.

Such thoughts were not original coming from Isabel, nor were they when first attributed to Jesus in Luke's Gospel or later reformulated by JFK. But certain ideas bear repeating, and McCall Smith is the master of refashioning tried and true maxims through the mouths of his pleasing and attractive characters, thereby reinforcing the endurance and vitality of old saws. I finished the book feeling well satisfied, morally chastened, and ready for more vigorous fare.

My month proceeded as had previous ones: more sobering works balanced with lighter-hearted volumes, mysteries tempered by coming-of-age novels, reflections on middle age or end of life harmonizing with literature for younger readers, gothic and noir countering memoir and exposition. I read short stories and longer novels, personal narratives and science fiction. I found pleasure in all of it.

I basked in the final words of the prologue in Thrity Umrigar's *Bombay Time* and turned the page eagerly to fill myself up with more: "A day, a day. A silver urn of promise and hope. Another chance. At reinvention, at resurrection, at reincarnation. A day. The least and most of our lives." My skin came up in goose bumps, my senses tensed and ready, in reading J. A.

Baker's limpid impressions of nature in *The Peregrine*: "As her wings swept up and back, she glided faster. And then faster, with her whole body flattened and compressed. Bending over in a splendid arc, she plunged to earth. . . . I saw fields flash up behind her; then she was gone beyond elms and hedges and farm buildings. And I was left with nothing but the wind blowing, the sun hidden, my neck and wrists cold and stiff, my eyes raw, and the glory gone."

My hope was raised to warming heights through the words of a main character in Sarah Hall's *How to Paint a Dead Man*, a heart-wrenching and life-affirming conclusion from a character who, for too long, had only contemplated death: "The world can accommodate your situation, as it accommodates all situations. And your body will keep explaining to you how it all works, this original experiment, this lifelong gift. Your body will keep describing how, for the time being at least, there is no escape from this particular vessel. These are your atoms. This is your consciousness. These are your experiences—your successes and mistakes. This is your first and final chance, your one and only biography. This is the existential container, the bowl of your life's soup, wherein something can be made sense of, wherein there is a cure, wherein you are."

I had spent a year mixing up the bowl of my life's soup, making a meal, seeking a cure, and finding myself. And accompanying my meal was a steady supply of books. After all, one of the simplest pleasures I know is to sit and eat with a book beside me, devouring words as I devour food. For at least one meal a week, I allow my kids to bring a book to the table and read while we eat. A shared meal, a shared pleasure.

The first home that Jack and I officially shared was a two-room fifth-floor walk-up on the Upper East Side. Just a few months after we moved in, I needed major knee surgery (the five-story walk-up was only partly to blame). After the surgery I was bedridden for almost three weeks, and hooked up to a knee machine that kept my left leg in constant motion. I couldn't leave the apartment, and because of the painkillers I was taking I had no appetite for food and was forbidden to drink. I couldn't fool around with Jack because that damn knee machine kept getting in the way. But I could read. For days and days at a time, all I did all day long was read. I discovered Jim Harrison, reading *The Woman Lit by Fireflies*; I read John Cheever and Leo Tolstoy and Barbara Kingsolver, and steeped in the stomach-dropping thrillers of Elizabeth George and the gentler mysteries of Antonia Fraser. I pawed my way through *The Quincunx* by Charles Palliser, a gift from Anne-Marie.

About one week into the recovery my leg swelled up to the size of a tree trunk (redwood), and the doctor told me to get myself down to the emergency room "now!"—i.e., immediately. Jack was out of town on business, and there was no way I could make it down five flights of stairs myself. I called Anne-Marie, who lived just four blocks away, and asked her to come get me, and to take me to the hospital.

"I'll be right there," she promised.

"Oh, and Anne-Marie, one more thing?"

"Yes, yes, anything."

"Could you just stop by the Corner Bookstore? They're holding David Leavitt's story collection *A Place I've Never Been* for me." I was lucky enough to live half a block from one of the best small bookstores in New York City, and its booksellers had supplied me during the past days with a steady stream of reading material.

"Nina, we have to get to the hospital! You could have a blood clot—this is serious."

"Yes, but I need something to read while I'm in there."

So Anne-Marie picked the book up for me and took me by cab down to NYU Hospital, and everything was fine. My leg shrank back down, the book was read, and I was happy.

When two more weeks passed and it was time for me to go back to work, I was not so happy. It wasn't that I didn't like my job. I worked then for the Natural Resources Defense Council, where I worked on sewage issues and where I was dubbed "the sludge queen"—what's not to love about a job like that? But I realized that now that I was going back to work, my days of uninterrupted hours of reading were coming to an end. I comforted myself with the knowledge that I'd have a long commute by bus (no way could I make it down the subway stairs on crutches) and could read on my way to and from work.

Now in my forties, I had resubmerged myself in a daily routine of hours spent reading. But I had added a new practice to the routine. I wrote about what I read, and I talked about books with anyone who wanted to talk with me. In sharing ideas and thoughts about what I was reading, I found a fundamental new satisfaction in books: talking about them.

Years earlier, in 1989, the *New Republic* published a commentary written by author and critic Irving Howe. Howe lamented the wide gap between literary critics and the reading public, whom he called "the common reader." He wrote that literary critics just don't care what "the common reader" is up to.

I wrote a letter in response to Howe's piece in which I stated that as a common reader myself, I didn't care much about what the literary critics were up to. Neither they nor their critiques had anything to do with the books I loved to read. When and if I did talk about books, it was not to discuss trends in narrative style or the latest critiques of text. Instead, "it's gossipy chatter akin to 'what's happening with the neighbors?' We love our books and we love the very real people who populate them."

In my letter I referenced an old movie by Maurice Pialat, *Loulou*, starring a young Gérard Depardieu in the title role. Loulou is a handsome young motorcycle-riding thug for whom a beautiful woman leaves her older, well-educated lover. As she hops on the back of the bike to ride away with Loulou, the older man calls out, "But you can't even talk about books with him!" She replies with disdain, "I read books, I don't have to talk about them."

To my surprise, the *New Republic* published my letter. To my even greater surprise, I met Irving Howe the following fall, at the offices of my physical therapist. I was there doing rehab for the knee, and he was an old man trying to keep his limbs and joints in working order. I introduced myself.

"Do I know you?" he asked, his eyes pinched over his glasses.

"I wrote the letter about being a common reader, in the *New Republic*."

He made a noise deep in his throat. "I guess we won't talk about books, then. I just hope you always keep reading them."

With that he turned away, back to his exercise bike. I never saw him again.

I was right about loving my books, but I had been wrong about not needing to talk about them. I was not like that young woman in *Loulou*. I do need to talk about books. Because talking about books allows me to talk about anything with anyone. With family, friends, and even with strangers who contacted me through my Web site (and became friends), when we discuss what we are reading, what we are really discussing is our own lives, our take on everything from sorrow to fidelity to responsibility, from money to religion, from worrying to inebriation, from sex to laundry, and back again. No topic is taboo, as long as we can tie it in to a book we've read, and all responses are allowed, couched in terms of characters and their situations.

On the last day of my year of reading I read Pete Dexter's *Spooner*. *Spooner* tells the story of two men, Calmer and Spooner, bound together by the love of a very difficult and bitter woman. Calmer is reserved, patient, and hardworking. His stepson Spooner is restless, reckless, and openhearted. Calmer leads Spooner to understand that every person is just one "part of the story," and by understanding the part Spooner plays, he can understand everything important, including how to work, how to teach, and how to love. When Spooner finds himself in the unlikely role of novelist, it is Calmer's example he follows: "There were two things Spooner absolutely knew about writing, and the first one was that you can't get away with pretending to care. The other one, if you're interested, is that nobody wants to hear what you dreamed about last night."

Very funny and engaging and moving. I read *Spooner* with pleasure. But I also found a mandate in that final book. I understood that I was "in the world . . . as part of the story" of everyone around me. My book-a-day project affected not only my life but those of everyone with whom I shared my reading. I spread the gratification of reading through discussing books, much as authors create bliss by writing them. What a gift, to share the joy and the comfort and the wisdom! Everything I shared, I found first through the simple act of sitting down in my purple chair and reading a book.

But there was still one more lesson to learn, and one more part of the story to be told.

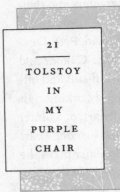

*Something had happened which was not noticed
by anyone, but which was much more important
than all that had been exposed to view.*

LEO TOLSTOY,
The Forged Coupon

MY FATHER SPENT TWO YEARS, TWO MONTHS, AND TWO DAYS
in a sanatorium. He was twenty-four years old the day he went
in and twenty-six when he came out again. While living and
studying in Regensburg, Germany, he had been accepted into
the University of Leuven's medical school in Belgium, winning
a place as a scholarship student. As part of the enrollment process all incoming students were required to undergo a physical
examination. X-rays of my father's chest showed spots on his
lungs, a dampness that indicated my father had tuberculosis.
His tuberculosis was a remnant of the war, a disease probably
contracted when living in refugee camps in southern Germany.
The examining doctors in Belgium told my father they would
arrange for him to get away from the city air of Leuven and up
to the healthy air of the open hills of Eupen. Medical school
would have to wait.

Eupen was a bucolic town set among meadows and forests
close to the border between Belgium and Germany. The sanatorium was housed in a huge stone building set up on a ridge
overlooking the surrounding hills and valleys. For the first two
months he spent at the sanatorium, my father was confined to

bed in a room he shared with another patient. After his health improved, he was allowed to join in the routine of the sanatorium, a monotonous rhythm of meals, socializing, and rest. Mornings were spent talking and reading. After an ample midday meal, my father spent the afternoons resting on a cot set out on the open verandas of the hospital, alongside dozens of other patients on cots. The patients rested under warm woolen blankets, basking in sun and the healing breezes coming down off the hills of the Hohes Venn to the south and the Aachener Wald to the north.

My father didn't know anyone at the sanatorium, but he slowly made friends among the strangers. One friend from Poland taught my father to play chess, and the two of them played for hours out on the veranda. Another friend, this one from Belgium, worked with my father on his French. Together my father and Charles deVries read novels out loud, and Charles helped my father with his articulation. My father still remembers that he learned how to pronounce the phrase "pince-nez" from reading Arthur Koestler's *Darkness at Noon*.

Some of the patients at the sanatorium died from their TB. Most, like my father, hung in there and survived. They improved their chess games, ate big meals of sustaining foods, rested after lunch on the veranda, and went to bed early every evening. Some patients were treated with antibiotics; others, less seriously ill like my father, were treated with pumps of air shot directly into their chests to cause lung collapse. Deprived of oxygen, the TB bacteria would die. The collapse allowed the lungs to reboot, like a computer turned off and then back on again.

In 1951 my father was deemed healthy and released from the sanatorium. He returned to Leuven and to medical school. One evening, while attending a lecture on theology and philosophy, my father first saw my mother. While the professor lectured on Saint Thomas Aquinas, my father sketched the profile of my mother in his notebook. After the lecture ended, my father approached my mother and introduced himself. My parents left the lecture hall together and went to a nearby café to play Ping-Pong. Six years later they were married, and seven years later, Anne-Marie was born.

My father's time in the sanatorium at Eupen was a pause in his life, a suspension of activity between war and peace. It was the hiatus between the murders of his sister and brothers, his forced separation from his parents and village, his months as a soldier and a refugee, and the next part of his life, the part in which he found my mother, moved to America, and welcomed the arrival, one by one, of his three girls. The second part of his life might not have come without the intervention of the two years, two months, and two days he spent at the sanatorium. His time there was his period of salvation not only from the tuberculosis but also from the wounds left by the war. He learned how to play chess and how to rest without a care in the world on a veranda under a blue sky. The time he spent taking care of his lungs was time he spent getting ready for the rest of his life, a strengthening of his body and his soul for the wonders still to come.

My father still plays chess almost every day in Central Park in New York City. In my parents' apartment, he usually has a game going on the chessboard set out in the living room, a game he plays against himself. When we were growing up, my father set up chess games after dinner, marking off moves on a wooden board in the study. During the day he played chess in the doctors' lounge at the hospital, in between operations and patient visits. I remember going along one Saturday morning and watching as a crowd of doctors gathered around my father and another doctor playing out a game of chess.

"Your daddy, he's good," one of the doctors told me. I knew that. He'd learned from great players, like the Polish patient waiting out the days alongside my father years ago in the Eupen sanatorium.

In Leo Tolstoy's novella *The Forged Coupon*, Tolstoy examines the twists and turns that one life takes, and the impact that one person can make on the life of another. The novella begins with a father, Fedor Mihailovich Smokovnikov, having a bad day at work. He comes home from the office and takes his bad day out on his family, first refusing to lend his son Mitia the money that Mitia needs to repay a loan and then being sullen and short-tempered at dinner: "The trio finished their dinner in silence, rose from the table, and separated, without a word."

Fedor's failure to lend his son a paltry sum, a seemingly minor act in the whole of Fedor's life, results in a cascade of actions and reactions affecting a huge and varied slew of characters. Mitia forges a coupon of payment (similar to a signed-over check) and passes it to a shopkeeper to get the money that he needs to repay his friend. When the shopkeeper discovers that the coupon he holds in his hand is a fraud, he plots his own deceit to get rid of the forged coupon, using it to pay for a load of wood from Ivan Mironov, a passing peasant. When the peasant attempts to use the coupon at a tavern, he is thrown into jail. Ivan pays a fine and, when released, seeks to redress the injustice by taking the shopkeeper to court. But the shopkeeper successfully bribes Vassily, a servant, to testify that no wood was ever bought from the peasant, and Ivan is told by the judge to pay court costs and get out.

Ivan, now destitute, turns to a life of crime, and steals the horses of Stepan Pelageushkine. The servant Vassily, sure now of the evilness of mankind, indulges in a life of thievery, even against his master, the shopkeeper. Mitia, having successfully pulled off the fraud, slides into a life of shallow materialism. Stepan, discovering that it was Ivan who stole his horses, kills Ivan with a stone, is sent to prison for one year, and comes out penniless and homeless. One by one the ripples of deceit and injustice spread, connecting previously unconnected lives in a course of greed, treachery, disillusionment, anger, and, eventually, murder.

The downward spiral of the actions and reactions is transformed, however, with the murder of a kindly older woman named Maria Semenovna. Just before she dies, she warns Stepan, her murderer, "Have mercy on yourself. To destroy somebody's soul . . . and worse, your own!" Stepan kills her anyway, but from the moment he draws the knife across her neck, he feels strange, and altered from the person he was before: "He felt suddenly so exhausted that he could not walk any farther. He stepped down into the gutter and remained there lying the rest of the night, and the next day, and the next night."

When Stepan finally gets up from the gutter, he goes straight to the police to turn himself in. In prison, Stepan begins to live his life as a form of redemption for the lives he has taken from others. He is kind to the other prisoners, compassionate to everyone, and touched with the gift of persuasion.

From this point on *The Forged Coupon* becomes a "pay it forward" story, wherein Stepan sets in motion a progression of goodness. Each good and generous act performed by a character is repaid in kind with an act of goodness toward another, and so the goodness passes along from person to person, and finally back to Mitia, the son who forged the coupon in the first place. Mitia meets Stepan and listens while the wizened man tells him of his life story. The story of Stepan's life transforms Mitia, "who up to that time used to spend his time drinking, eating, and gambling" but now changes his life. He buys an estate, marries, and devotes himself "to the peasantry, helping them as much as he could." Mitia, who had been estranged from his father, goes to see him to make up for the past. Old Fedor, greatly moved, realizes the goodness that lies in his son, and in himself.

It was only at the very end of my year of reading that I understood the story Tolstoy tells in *The Forged Coupon*. Back in July, when I first read it, I understood the message about how we are all connected, and how one action sets off a chain reaction of impacts and consequences. But now, sitting back in my purple chair and remembering *The Forged Coupon*, I realized that Tolstoy was laying out an explanation for everything that had happened to me, and setting forth the meaning of my life. The events I had experienced—dodgeball on the front lawn on summer nights, travels with my parents, being pulled off the wrong bus by my sister, ramming into the cop car, all the times I'd fallen in love, the birth of my children, the death of my sister—set the contours of my life. But the meaning of my life is ultimately defined by how I respond to the joys and the sorrows, how I forge crossbars of connection and experience, and how I extend help to others as they travel on their own winding road of existence.

My year of reading one book a day was my year in a sanatorium. It was my year away from the unhealthy air of anger and grief with which I'd filled my life. It was an escape into the healing breezes of hills of books. My year of reading was my own hiatus, my own suspension in time between the overwhelming sorrow of my sister's death and the future that now waits before me. During my yearlong respite filled with books, I recuperated. Even more, I learned how to move beyond recuperation to living.

When I ran from the hospital room where Anne-Marie died, the room where I last saw her alive and kissed her and told her, with confidence, that I would see her again tomorrow, I was running away. Running away from that room where I found my parents destroyed by grief and Natasha sobbing, where Marvin paced the room manically and Jack tried to comfort us all.

For three years I had run as fast as I could, trying to live and love and learn at double speed to make up for what Anne-Marie had lost. Trying to anesthetize myself from what I'd lost. When I decided to read a book a day and write about it, I'd finally stopped running away. I sat down, sat still, and started to read. Every day I read and devoured and digested and thought about all the books, their authors, their characters, and their conclusions. I immersed myself in the world the authors had created, and I witnessed new ways of handling the twists and turns of life, discovering tools of humor and empathy and connection. Through my reading, I reached the point of understanding so much.

My life would not be constrained by how my sister died but could only be amplified by how she had lived. Her place in my life is defined by everything that she did, everything she showed me, and the way she led me to new ideas.

The summer after I graduated from college, I went to visit Anne-Marie in New York City. She was subletting an apartment in Chelsea for the summer, the top floor of a brownstone. Chelsea was still on the edge then, a mix of newly arrived upwardly mobile types and a solid lower middle class that had lived there for decades, fringed by a seedier element of SRO occupants, drunks, and drug dealers.

Anne-Marie had just started things up with Marvin, and I had fallen in love with the manager of the ice-cream store where I worked in Harvard Square. But during our weekend together, we didn't talk about the men in our lives. We talked about the church Anne-Marie studied, Saint-Eustache in Paris, and how beautiful its arches were, its decorative flourishes and its imposing facade. We talked about the short stories of Ann Beattie, whose apartment Anne-Marie was subletting, and our conflicting reactions to her writing (we both loved her apartment). Anne-Marie allowed that I was still too young to like Beattie's stories but that I would, one day. We talked about what I should do with a law degree, pursue my interest in history or start a political career. Anne-Marie was sure I'd make a good senator.

On Saturday evening, early still with plenty of light left before the sun went down, we climbed out through a window of the apartment onto the tarred roof of the brownstone. The black surface was squishy beneath our feet, and warm. We perched on the stone parapet edges of the roof and looked out over New York City. We could see the Empire State Building rising above a maze of roofs and water towers. We took Polaroids of each other. In the photos, which I have still, we are young and healthy, skinny in our tight white T-shirts and our short shorts, and we are smiling, looking vigorous and confident. We stayed out on the roof as the sky darkened into a deep purple. We must have eaten dinner at some point, but I don't remember that. I just remember sitting beside her, the lights of New York City going on all around us, and talking late into the night.

Anne-Marie was right in predicting that I would grow to appreciate the writer Ann Beattie, but everything else that happened, we could never have foreseen: how Anne-Marie would write about Saint-Eustache in a whole new way of looking at architecture; how I would become a working lawyer, leaving both history and politics behind, and then become a mother, leaving law behind; how Anne-Marie and Marvin would become godparents to the third of my four boys; how one January morning, just twenty years after our evening out on the roof, Anne-Marie would feel a lump in her abdomen; and how four months after that, she would die.

Tolstoy wrote, "The sole meaning of life is to serve humanity." He understood this service as a religious duty. For me, I understand it as a fact of life, as *the* fact of life, and as the sustaining fact of life. What we do for each other is what survives. My sister is dead, but everything she did for me while she was alive is still going strong. I can still feel her hand reaching across the backseat of our car in Berlin, and I still hear her voice, our conversations going late into the night.

Anne-Marie is defined by everything that she was to me, as oldest sister, scholar, beauty, friend. She is the way I worshipped her and bugged her and loved her. My life is a reflection of her life. I will anchor myself with her life, and not with her death. Death took all choices away from her, but not from me, and I choose to live on with her beside me always, alive in all my memories of how she lived. She will continue to shape me, direct me, and advise me. She pulled me toward my year of reading a book a day, spurring me on with our shared love of books and my desire to read all the volumes upon volumes that we might have read together.

I have learned, through books, to hold on to my memories of all the beautiful moments and people in my life, as I need those memories to help me through difficult times. I have learned to allow forgiveness, both of myself and of people around me, all trying with "their heavy burden" just to get by. I know now that love is a power great enough to survive death, and that kindness is the greatest connector between me and the rest of the world. Most important—because I know now that Anne-Marie will always be with me, and with everyone she loved—I understand the lasting impact that one life can have on another, and another, and another.

There is no remedy for the sorrow of losing someone we love, nor should there be. Sorrow is not an illness or an affliction. It is the only response possible to the death of a loved one, and an affirmation of just how much we value life itself, for all its wonder and thrill and beauty and satisfaction.

Our only answer to sorrow is to live. To live looking backward, remembering the ones we have lost, but also moving forward, with anticipation and excitement. And to pass on those feelings of hope and possibility through acts of kindness, generosity, and compassion.

My whole life, I have read books. And when I needed to read the most, books gave me everything I asked for and more. My year of reading gave me the space I needed to figure out how to live again after losing my sister. My year in the sanatorium of books allowed me to redefine what is important for me and what can be left behind. Not all respites from life can be so all-consuming—I will never again read a book a day for one year—but any break taken from the frenetic pace of busy days can restore the balance of a life turned topsy-turvy. For some people it will be an afternoon spent knitting or the weekly yoga class or a long walk with a friend or a leashed animal. We all need a space to just let things be, a place to remember who we are and what is important to us, an interval of time that allows the happiness and joy of living back into our consciousness.

"We live in wonder, blaze in a cycle of passion and apprehension," wrote the poet Carolyn Kizer, and I know that to be true. My hiatus is over, my soul and my body are healed, but I will never leave the purple chair for long. So many books waiting to be read, so much happiness to be found, so much wonder to be revealed.

ACKNOWLEDGMENTS

My heartfelt thanks to my parents, Tilde and Anatole Sankovitch, and my sister Natasha, for their constancy and company and love.

Thank-you to my in-laws Pat and Bob Menz, and to all of my brothers- and sisters-in-law, for their unfailing faith in me; to Joan Batten, for all her great ideas; to my children, Peter, Michael, George, and Martin, for filling my life with light; to my stepdaughter, Meredith, for allowing me to be her oldest friend; and to all the Janssens, for sharing books and family stories and long meals.

Thanks to Jack Menz, for being who and what he is, which is everything to me.

Thank-you to Stephanie Young, Margaret Kelley, Sally Maca, Bev Stanley, Sarah Hickson, Christine Utter, Viveca Van Bladel, Nataliya Lenskiy, Tish Fried, David and Laura Wilk, Gary Ginsberg, Joe Tringali, Margaret Hughes Henderson, Susan Paullin Nussbaum, Marion Nixon, Kate Sheehan Gerlach, Ellice Ratliff, Kristina Krause, Angie Atkins, Celia Zahner, and Jill Owens. Special thanks to Debbie Holm and Catherine Jacobi of Ted Studios. Thank-you to Tim and Patsy Wallace and to Peter Applebome. Thank-you to Tazewell Thompson, who showed me that dedication plus desire creates things of beauty.

I could never have found all the wonderful books I did during my year of reading without the resources of the Westport Public Library. I owe special thanks to Marta Campbell, who finds books from all over the world and brings them home to Westport.

Thank you a million times over to Esther Newberg, for giving me confidence, and to Julia Cheiffetz and Katie Salisbury, for pushing me onward, with patient determination.

I offer thanks and reverence to all the great authors I've read during the past forty-plus years and from whom I hope to keep drawing wisdom, comfort, pleasure, escape, and joy until my last breath.

COMPLETE LIST OF BOOKS READ

FROM OCTOBER 28, 2008,

TO OCTOBER 28, 2009

———

*After so much had been taken,
so much could still be received.*

TATJANA SOLI,
The Lotus Eaters

The Abbot's Ghost, by Louisa May Alcott
About Schmidt, by Louis Begley
Act of the Damned, by António Lobo Antunes
Address Unknown, by Kathrine Kressmann Taylor
The African Queen, by C. S. Forester
The Age of Dreaming, by Nina Revoyr
Algren at Sea, by Nelson Algren
Alice Fantastic, by Maggie Estep
All My Friends Are Superheroes, by Andrew
   Kaufman
All Souls, by Christine Schutt
All That I Have, by Castle Freeman Jr.
American Born Chinese, by Gene Luen Yang
Amphibian, by Carla Gunn
The Ancient Shore, by Shirley Hazzard and Francis
   Steegmuller
Anna In-Between, by Elizabeth Nunez
Annie John, by Jamaica Kincaid
Are You Somebody? by Nuala O'Faolain
The Art of Racing in the Rain, by Garth Stein

The Assault, by Harry Mulisch
Aunt Dimity Slays the Dragon, by Nancy Atherton
Bangkok Haunts, by John Burdett
Beauty Salon, by Mario Bellatin
The Believers, by Zoë Heller
Bellwether, by Connie Willis
The Best Place to Be, by Lesley Dormen
Better, by John O'Brien
Bird by Bird, by Anne Lamott
Black Water, by Joyce Carol Oates
Blank, by Noah Tall
The Body Artist, by Don DeLillo
Bombay Time, by Thrity Umrigar
The Book of Chameleons, by José Eduardo Agualusa
The Book of Murder, by Guillermo Martínez
Boston Noir, edited by Dennis Lehane
Breath, Eyes, Memory, by Edwidge Danticat
The Bridge of San Luis Rey, by Thornton Wilder
The Bridges at Toko-Ri, by James A. Michener
Brief Encounters with Che Guevara, by Ben Fountain
The Brief Wondrous Life of Oscar Wao, by Junot Díaz
Brooklyn, by Colm Tóibín
By Chance, by Martin Corrick
Bye, Bye Soccer, by Edilberto Coutinho
The Calling, by Mary Gray Hughes
Call Me Ahab, by Anne Finger
Camera, by Jean-Philippe Toussaint
Captains Courageous, by Rudyard Kipling
Castle Nowhere, by Constance Fenimore Woolson
The Castle of Otranto, by Horace Walpole
A Celibate Season, by Carol Shields and Blanche
    Howard
Charles Dickens, by Melisa Klimaszewski and Melissa
    Gregory
Cheese, by Willem Elsschot
Christmas in Plains, by Jimmy Carter

Climate of Fear, by Wole Soyinka
Conjugal Love, by Alberto Moravia
Consider the Lobster, by David Foster Wallace
Cooking and Screaming, by Adrienne Kane
The Council of the Cursed, by Peter Tremayne
The Crofter and the Laird, by John McPhee
Crow Planet, by Lyanda Lynn Haupt
Crusader's Cross, by James Lee Burke
The Crying of Lot 49, by Thomas Pynchon
The Curriculum Vitae of Aurora Ortiz, by Almudena
    Solana
The Curse of Eve, by Liliana Blum
A Curtain of Green, by Eudora Welty
Dangerous Games, by Margaret MacMillan
Dangerous Laughter, by Steven Millhauser
The Darts of Cupid, by Edith Templeton
Dead Giveaway, by Simon Brett
Dead Horse, by Walter Satterthwait
A Dead Man in Barcelona, by Michael Pearce
Deaf Sentence, by David Lodge
Death Etc., by Harold Pinter
Death of a Witch, by M. C. Beaton
Death Rites, by Alicia Giménez-Bartlett
Death with Interruptions, by José Saramago
The Deer Leap, by Martha Grimes
DeKok and Murder by Installment, by A. C. Baantjer
Delhi Noir, edited by Hirsh Sawhney
Desperate Characters, by Paula Fox
The Detective Wore Silk Drawers, by Peter Lovesey
The Devil's Tickets, by Gary M. Pomerantz
The Diamond Girls, by Jacqueline Wilson
The Diary of a Nobody, by George and Weedon
    Grossmith
Disquiet, by Julia Leigh
Divisadero, by Michael Ondaatje
Dogs, Dreams, and Men, by Joan Kaufman

The Door to Bitterness, by Martin Limón
Double-Click for Trouble, by Chris Woodworth
Dreamers, by Knut Hamsun
Drink to Yesterday, by Manning Coles
The Duppy, by Anthony C. Winkler
The Elegance of the Hedgehog, by Muriel Barbery
The Emigrants, by W. G. Sebald
Emma-Jean Lazarus Fell in Love, by Lauren Tarshis
The Emperor's Tomb, by Joseph Roth
Ender's Game, by Orson Scott Card
The English Major, by Jim Harrison
Escape Under the Forever Sky, by Eve Yohalem
Esther's Inheritance, by Sándor Márai
Even Cat Sitters Get the Blues, by Blaize Clement
Ex Libris, by Anne Fadiman
Explorers of the New Century, by Magnus Mills
Facing the Bridge, by Yoko Tawada
The Fairacre Festival, by Miss Read
The Faithful Lover, by Massimo Bontempelli
The Fall, by Albert Camus
Falling Angels, by Tracy Chevalier
Family Happiness, by Laurie Colwin
The Famous Flower of Serving Men, by Deborah Grabien
Female Trouble, by Antonya Nelson
The Ferguson Affair, by Ross Macdonald
Fiendish Deeds, by P. J. Bracegirdle
The Fifth Child, by Doris Lessing
Fight Scenes, by Greg Bottoms
Fine Just the Way It Is, by Annie Proulx
The First Person, by Ali Smith
A Fisherman of the Inland Sea, by Ursula K. Le Guin
The Forged Coupon, by Leo Tolstoy
For Grace Received, by Valeria Parrella
Forty Stories, by Donald Barthelme
Frida's Bed, by Slavenka Drakulić

Colum   Goodbye w/out Leaving

The Garden Party, by Katherine Mansfield

Gerard Keegan's Famine Diary, by James J. Mangan

The German Mujahid, by Boualem Sansal

Girl Boy Girl, by Savannah Knoop

The Glass Castle, by Jeannette Walls

Godlike, by Richard Hell

Gold, by Dan Rhodes

Good Behaviour, by Molly Keane

The Good Life According to Hemingway, by A. E. Hotchner

The Good Soldier, by Ford Madox Ford

The Good Thief, by Hannah Tinti

The Granny, by Brendan O'Carroll

A Great Day for a Ballgame, by Fielding Dawson

Grief, by Andrew Holleran

The Grotesque, by Patrick McGrath

The Guernsey Literary and Potato Peel Pie Society, by Mary Ann Shaffer and Annie Barrows

The Gutter and the Grave, by Ed McBain

Hairstyles of the Damned, by Joe Meno

Half in Love, by Maile Meloy

Hannah Coulter, by Wendell Berry

Happens Every Day, by Isabel Gillies

A Happy Marriage, by Rafael Yglesias

The Haunted Man and the Ghost's Bargain, by Charles Dickens

Her Deadly Mischief, by Beverle Graves Myers

The History of Love, by Nicole Krauss

The Hollow-Eyed Angel, by Janwillem van de Wetering

A Hope in the Unseen, by Ron Suskind

The House Beautiful, by Allison Burnett

The Housekeeper and the Professor, by Yoko Ogawa

Housekeeping vs. the Dirt, by Nick Hornby

The House on Eccles Road, by Judith Kitchen

How I Became a Nun, by César Aira

The Howling Miller, by Arto Paasilinna
How to Paint a Dead Man, by Sarah Hall
The Hunt for Sonya Dufrette, by R. T. Raichev
I Feel Bad About My Neck, by Nora Ephron
I Love Dollars, by Zhu Wen
Indignation, by Philip Roth
In Her Absence, by Antonio Muñoz Molina
Inkheart, by Cornelia Funke
The Inner Game of Tennis, by W. Timothy Gallwey
In the Meantime, by Robin Lippincott
In the Pond, by Ha Jin
In the Woods, by Tana French
In Time of Peace, by Thomas Boyd
Iron Balloons, edited by Colin Channer
I Was Dora Suarez, by Derek Raymond
Jacob's Hands, by Aldous Huxley and Christopher
    Isherwood
Jerusalem, by Selma Lagerlöf
John Crow's Devil, by Marlon James
The Joys of Motherhood, by Buchi Emecheta
Kindred, by Octavia E. Butler
The King and the Cowboy, by David Fromkin
Kitchen, by Banana Yoshimoto
Krapp's Last Cassette, by Anne Argula
Lark and Termite, by Jayne Anne Phillips
The Last Essays of Elia, by Charles Lamb
Last Night at the Lobster, by Stewart O'Nan
The Laughter of Dead Kings, by Elizabeth Peters
Laura Rider's Masterpiece, by Jane Hamilton
The Law of Similars, by Chris Bohjalian
The Laws of Evening, by Mary Yukari Waters
A Lesson Before Dying, by Ernest J. Gaines
Letter to a Christian Nation, by Sam Harris
Life on the Refrigerator Door, by Alice Kuipers
Little Bee, by Chris Cleave
The Little Disturbances of Man, by Grace Paley

The Loneliness of the Long-Distance Runner, by Alan
 Sillitoe
The Lost Art of Gratitude, by Alexander McCall Smith
The Lost Prophecies, by C. J. Sansom, Bernard Knight,
 Ian Morson, Michael Jecks, Susanna Gregory, and
 Philip Gooden
Love and Death, by Forrest Church
The Loved One, by Evelyn Waugh
The Love of the Last Tycoon, by F. Scott Fitzgerald
The Love Song of Monkey, by Michael Graziano
Love Walked In, by Marisa de los Santos
Madame de Staël, by Francine du Plessix Gray
Make No Bones, by Aaron Elkins
Man in the Dark, by Paul Auster
The Man in the Picture, by Susan Hill
The Man of My Life, by Manuel Vázquez Montalbán
The Man Who Was Thursday, by G. K. Chesterton
Marley and Me, by John Grogan
The Master of Petersburg, by J. M. Coetzee
Masterpiece, by Elise Broach
Meat Eaters and Plant Eaters, by Jessica Treat
A Mercy, by Toni Morrison
The Mercy Papers, by Robin Romm
Miss Lonelyhearts, by Nathanael West
Miss Misery, by Andy Greenwald
Mister Pip, by Lloyd Jones
The Moon Opera, by Bi Feiyu
Moon Tiger, by Penelope Lively
Murder in the Calais Coach, by Agatha Christie
Murder Is My Racquet, edited by Otto Penzler
The Musical Illusionist, by Alex Rose
My House in Umbria, by William Trevor
Narrative of the Life of Frederick Douglass, by Frederick
 Douglass
Never Let Me Go, by Kazuo Ishiguro
Newton, by Peter Ackroyd

The Nick Adams Stories, by Ernest Hemingway
Nobody Move, by Denis Johnson
The Notebooks of Malte Laurids Brigge, by Rainer
    Maria Rilke
Nothing to Be Frightened Of, by Julian Barnes
Oh Joe, by Michael Z. Lewin
The Old Man and Me, by Elaine Dundy
Olive Kitteridge, by Elizabeth Strout
On Chesil Beach, by Ian McEwan
One Dog Happy, by Molly McNett
One Foot in Eden, by Ron Rash
Onitsha, by J. M. G. Le Clézio
On Kindness, by Adam Phillips and Barbara Taylor
On the Line, by Serena Williams with Daniel Paisner
On the Pleasure of Hating, by William Hazlitt
The Open Door, by Elizabeth Maguire
The Orchid Shroud, by Michelle Wan
Out of Captivity, by Marc Gonsalves, Keith Stansell,
    and Tom Howes with Gary Brozek
The Palestinian Lover, by Sélim Nassib
Pastoralia, by George Saunders
The Patience of the Spider, by Andrea Camilleri
Payback, by Margaret Atwood
People of the Book, by Geraldine Brooks
The Peregrine, by J. A. Baker
The Perfectionists, by Gail Godwin
Petey & Pussy, by John Kerschbaum
The Picts and the Martyrs, by Arthur Ransome
Pilate's Wife, by H.D.
The Pisstown Chaos, by David Ohle
The Plated City, by Bliss Perry
Please Kill Me, by Legs McNeil and Gillian McCain
Poisonville, by Massimo Carlotto and Marco Videtta
Polaris, by Fay Weldon
The Poorhouse Fair, by John Updike
Pressure Is a Privilege, by Billie Jean King

The Private Patient, by P. D. James
The Provincial Lady in London, by E. M. Delafield
The Public Prosecutor, by Jef Geeraerts
Pulpy and Midge, by Jessica Westhead
The Pursuit of Love, by Nancy Mitford
Rage, by Sergio Bizzio
Rancho Weirdo, by Laura Chester
Respected Sir, by Naguib Mahfouz
Revelation, by C. J. Sansom
Revolutionary Road, by Richard Yates
Rhino Ranch, by Larry McMurtry
Rimbaud, by Edmund White
River of Darkness, by Rennie Airth
A Rogue's Life, by Wilkie Collins
Rome Noir, edited by Chiara Stangalino and Maxim
    Jakubowski
Ronald Reagan, by Andrew Helfer, illustrated by
    Steve Buccellato and Joe Staton
Roseanna, by Maj Sjöwall and Per Wahlöö
Ruins, by Achy Obejas
The Rules of Engagement, by Anita Brookner
Russian Journal, by Andrea Lee
The Salt-Box House, by Jane de Forest Shelton
Salvation and Other Disasters, by Josip Novakovich
The Samurai's Garden, by Gail Tsukiyama
Say You're One of Them, by Uwem Akpan
Scat, by Carl Hiaasen
Seize the Day, by Saul Bellow
Self's Murder, by Bernhard Schlink
The Servants' Quarters, by Lynn Freed
The Session, by Aaron Petrovich
The Seven Deadly Sins, edited by Angus Wilson
Sex, Drugs, and Cocoa Puffs, by Chuck Klosterman
The Shadow of the Sun, by Ryszard Kapuściński
A Short History of Women, by Kate Walbert
Silks, by Dick Francis and Felix Francis

Silverwing, by Kenneth Oppel

The Simulacra, by Philip K. Dick

The Sin Eater, by Alice Thomas Ellis

Six Early Stories, by Thomas Mann

Six Kinds of Sky, by Luis Alberto Urrea

The Sixth Target, by James Patterson and Maxine
    Paetro

The Skating Rink, by Roberto Bolaño

The Slippery Year, by Melanie Gideon

Smile as They Bow, by Nu Nu Yi

A Smile of Fortune, by Joseph Conrad

Snakehead, by Anthony Horowitz

Something Nasty in the Woodshed, by Kyril Bonfiglioli

Somewhere Towards the End, by Diana Athill

Songs My Mother Never Taught Me, by Selçuk Altun

Son of Holmes, by John Lescroart

Speak, by Laurie Halse Anderson

The Spoke, by Friedrich Glauser

Spooner, by Pete Dexter

A Sport and a Pastime, by James Salter

Stardust, by Neil Gaiman

Stitches, by David Small

Stolen Children, by Peg Kehret

The Sun Field, by Heywood Broun

A Sun for the Dying, by Jean-Claude Izzo

The Swap, by Antony Moore

Tamburlaine Must Die, by Louise Welsh

The Tempest Tales, by Walter Mosley

Ten Poems to Set You Free, by Roger Housden

A Terrible Splendor, by Marshall Jon Fisher

The Thanksgiving Visitor, by Truman Capote

They Who Do Not Grieve, by Sia Figiel

The Thing Around Your Neck, by Chimamanda Ngozi
    Adichie

Things Fall Apart, by Chinua Achebe

The Third Angel, by Alice Hoffman

The Thirty-Nine Steps, by John Buchan
The Three of Us, by Julia Blackburn
A Toast to Tomorrow, by Manning Coles
The Tomb in Seville, by Norman Lewis
To Siberia, by Per Petterson
The Touchstone, by Edith Wharton
Towards the End of the Morning, by Michael Frayn
Twenty Boy Summer, by Sarah Ockler
Twice-Told Tales, by Nathaniel Hawthorne
Twilight, by Stephenie Meyer
Two Marriages, by Phillip Lopate
Under the Frangipani, by Mia Couto
The Unknown Masterpiece, by Honoré de Balzac
Vanessa and Virginia, by Susan Sellers
The Vengeance of the Witch-Finder, by John Bellairs,
    completed by Brad Strickland
The Venice Train, by Georges Simenon
The Vicar of Sorrows, by A. N. Wilson
Victorian Tales of Terror, edited by Hugh Lamb
Waiting in Vain, by Colin Channer
Wake, by Lisa McMann
Walk the Blue Fields, by Claire Keegan
War Dances, by Sherman Alexie
Watchmen, by Alan Moore and Dave Gibbons
Watership Down, by Richard Adams
The Weekend, by Peter Cameron
What I'd Say to the Martians, by Jack Handey
What I Talk About When I Talk About Running, by
    Haruki Murakami
When You Are Engulfed in Flames, by David Sedaris
Where Angels Fear to Tread, by E. M. Forster
Where the Money Went, by Kevin Canty
Where Three Roads Meet, by John Barth
Where You Once Belonged, by Kent Haruf
The White Tiger, by Aravind Adiga
The Whore's Child, by Richard Russo

Willful Behavior, by Donna Leon
Will War Ever End? by Paul K. Chappell
Will Work for Drugs, by Lydia Lunch
Winning Ugly, by Brad Gilbert and Steve Jamison
Wizard's Hall, by Jane Yolen
The Wright 3, by Blue Balliett
The Writing Life, by Annie Dillard
The Yellow Leaves, by Frederick Buechner
The Yellow Wallpaper, by Charlotte Perkins Gilman

PERMISSIONS

Grateful acknowledgment is made to the following authors and works for excerpts used herein; it is only by reading the complete text of these books that their full beauty and importance can be appreciated:

ABOUT THE AUTHOR

Douglas Healey

The youngest of three girls, **Nina Sankovitch** was born in Evanston, Illinois, to immigrant parents. She graduated from Tufts University and Harvard Law School. She worked as a corporate lawyer and later as a coastal attorney with the Natural Resources Defense Council and became executive director of Save the Sound in 2003. In 2008, Nina launched ReadAllDay.org, and at the end of her year of reading, she was profiled in the *New York Times*. She continues to review books on ReadAllDay.org and for the *Huffington Post*. She lives in Connecticut with her husband and four sons.